Hellebores

Hellebores

Graham Rice

MITCHELL BEAZLEY

THE ROYAL HORTICULTURAL SOCIETY

Hellebores
Graham Rice

First published in Great Britain in 2003 by Cassell Illustrated, an imprint
of Octopus Publishing Group Limited.
This edition published in 2008 in association with the Royal
Horticultural Society by Mitchell Beazley, an imprint of Octopus
Publishing Group Limited, 2–4 Heron Quays, London E14 4JP
An Hachette Livre UK Company
www.octopusbooks.co.uk

A CIP catalogue record for this book is available from the
British Library.

ISBN 978 1 84533 381 2

Commissioning Editor Camilla Stoddart
Art Editor Justin Hunt
Designer Martin Hendry

Set in Bembo

Colour reproduction by Dot Gradations Ltd.
Printed and bound by Toppan in China

CONTENTS

Title Page:
The Orientalis
Hybrids, Helleborus
hybridus, *come in an*
increasingly wide range
of colours – with and
without spots.

INTRODUCTION

We all need sparks of relief from the dull days of winter. Autumn colour has faded, the leaves have fallen and spring bulbs are hardly beginning, so the flowers of hellebores are especially welcome when there is so little else to enjoy in our chilly borders. But the hellebores are always there. Among the toughest and most resilient of all perennials, their flowers come in the most varied of colours and flower forms. And even though they bow their heads to the icy soil on frosty mornings, as the sun warms their juicy stems, their heads rise and glow and provide colour for us to admire as well as nectar for the first adventurous bees of the season.

Their foliage too, almost universally evergreen, is attractive even before the flowers are open. It provides a boldness and structure in winter, especially when prettily rimmed in morning frost. There are other attractions. Some species are tall, over a metre (3ft) high, with a boldness of impact during summer and autumn that allows the creative gardener to develop striking associations. As the display matures in late winter and spring, hundreds of flowers may open on a single plant. Seedlings are readily self-sown around established plants and they provide surprises when they flower. Their resilience in less than ideal growing conditions is welcome when so many choice plants require more cosseting.

The delicate patterning of the flowers even captivates observers with no horticultural interest. Turn up a flower of one of the spotted forms of the Lenten rose, *Helleborus hybridus*, or one of the crimson-streaked green flowers of *H. torquatus*, and

Rimmed in frost, the foliage of the Corsican hellebore, Helleborus arguitfolius, *makes a fine winter feature even before the green flowers open.*

the surprising interior of the flower is delicately patterned. The pure white Christmas rose, *H. niger*, is the classic Christmas card hellebore, but there are many more hellebores in many more colours for gardeners to enjoy, as this book will reveal.

A BRIEF OVERVIEW OF HELLEBORES

Hellebores belong to the genus *Helleborus* and are members of the buttercup family, Ranunculaceae. There are 16 wild species and five hybrid species. Just two species, *H. foetidus* and *H. viridis*, grow naturally in Britain, with other species distributed eastwards across central and southern Europe, including the Iberian peninsula and some Mediterranean islands. The greatest concentration of species occurs in countries around the Baltic Sea, and their range also extends along the Black Sea coast of Turkey and into Russia. It is slightly surprising that there are also two species that grow very separately from this main range: the very distinctive *H. vesicarius* grows on the border between Syria and Turkey, while *H. thibetanus* grows even farther afield in China.

British species, in particular *H. foetidus*, have long been grown in gardens for their medicinal value. Hellebores are poisonous and may cause skin irritation when touched, and a few gardeners need to wear gloves when working with them, even when cleaning seed. If eaten, they produce a range of unpleasant symptoms, such as vomiting and paralysis, but have also been used to treat psychiatric disorders, especially 'melancholike', as a diuretic, and to treat intestinal worms. It is important to stress the dangers of eating hellebores; the roots are the most potent, and gardeners should take care not to discard foliage and stems where grazing animals may eat them. For instance, do not throw cut foliage over your fence into a field as there are recent records of animals being poisoned by eating hellebore leaves.

Showy species from relatively nearby have also long been cultivated: *Helleborus niger*, also valued medicinally, since ancient Greek times, *H. argutifolius* since at least 1625 and *H. orientalis* from 1841. Much more recently, seed of *H. thibetanus* was introduced from China in 1991.

THE NATURE OF HELLEBORES

Sweeping generalizations about the habitat of hellebores can be misleading. A few species grow naturally in open, sunny and often rather dry and stony situations. Rather more species appreciate shade, but rarely the dense, unbroken shade of mature woodland. They are more often found in woodland clearings and along woodland edges, in open scrub, on the shady side of hedgerows. They are also found growing wild in meadows exposed to full light in winter and early spring, but the tall grasses cast shade over them in the height of summer.

Almost all hellebores are evergreen perennials, although the extent to which they retain their leaves often depends on the severity of the winter. Most are long-lived, producing flower stems and foliage separately from a slowly expanding, tough and rather woody rootstock. A few, known as caulescent hellebores, have upright woody stems that carry the foliage and are topped with clusters of flowers; as the stems extend and more leaves develop, the first leaves at the base dry up and may drop off. Caulescent hellebores tend to be much shorter lived.

It is conventional to divide wild hellebores into two groups; the acaulescent group (literally: without stems) and the caulescent group. The latter group includes species with obvious stems – *H. argutifolius*, *H. foetidus*, *H.* × *sternii* and *H. lividus* – and the acaulescent group includes all the others. More recent research reveals that the separation of hellebores into these two groups may be too simplistic. While it is a very convenient distinction from the gardener's point of view, it seems more likely that many apparently acaulescent species do in fact have dramatically contracted stems from which the leaves and flowers spring, but so much reduced as not to be immediately obvious.

In most species, leaves and flowering shoots spring from the tip of a dense rhizome, from where the youngest and most active white roots also develop. Older roots, further back on the rhizome, are black and serve more to anchor the plant than to gather moisture and nutrients. The necessity of water and nutrient uptake is restricted to the newer white roots, which have noticeable hairs towards their tips. All the roots are fat and stringy.

In general, the leaves are 'pedate'. Each one is split into a number of divisions at the point where it joins the stem, and those divisions are themselves divided. Some leaves have just three leaflets, others are repeatedly divided and so may have over a hundred slender divisions. Just one species, *H. vesicarius*, has leaves both arising from the rootstock and carried on the flower stems; this most distinctive hellebore also has impressively inflated seed pods.

HELLEBORE FLOWERS

It is immediately obvious that hellebore flowers are generally similar to the familiar buttercups of fields and roadsides. Their closest relatives, however, are actually the winter aconite, *Eranthis hyemalis* (in which the organization of the flowers is almost identical even if other features are not) and perhaps *Nigella,* love-in-a-mist.

The flower structure of hellebores has developed in a very

The unique inflated fruits of Helleborus vesicarius *are blown around the dry hillsides of its native habitat so the seeds can be widely distributed.*

particular way in response to the early flowering season of the wild species. The flowers of many wild hellebores are relatively dull in colouring, with green or dowdy brownish or purplish tones – not the most striking attractants for pollinating insects. When hellebores flower early in the year, bumble bees, honey bees and various solitary bees, which pollinate the flowers, are relatively scarce. In a measured evolutionary response to the need for pollinators, therefore, the petals of the hellebores have evolved into nectaries, since nectar serves as an effective and vital reward to pollinating insects on their first chilly spring flights.

The nectaries around the centre of the flower are short and tubular, and generally green or yellow. In a parallel development, and in order to shelter the sexual parts of the flower and provide a little colour (white or pink in some species), there has been another change: the sepals, whose function in most flowers is to protect the petals and sexual organs in bud, have evolved into larger, more showy and colourful organs. In effect, the sepals have taken on the shape and function of petals, and the petals have taken on the shape and function of nectaries. The sepals are sometimes referred to as petaloid sepals or 'tepals', but here I use the word petal since hellebore sepals look like petals to gardeners, if not to botanists. In some cultivars, the nectaries revert to their origins as true petals, and in such cases the flowers have petals as well as sepals; these are called double flowers.

So a typical hellebore flower consists of five large, coloured, usually slightly overlapping 'petals', which make a flower anything from 2–10cm (¾–4in) in diameter. These surround a ring of up to about 30 short, tubular nectaries, which are usually yellowish, honey coloured or green, sometimes marked in purple. Within the ring of nectaries is a ring of stamens, the male parts of the flower. Sometimes these number over 100, with yellow pollen bursting from the anthers at the top of slender filaments. These, in turn, surround the carpels.

Endangered in the wild, the Majorcan Helleborus lividus is well established in gardens and is a superb winter plant for frost free conditions.

The carpels are the female parts of the flower; there can be one or two, or up to almost a dozen, often depending on the overall health and vigour of the individual plant as well as the tendency of a specific species. Each carpel consists of an upright pouch of ovules, which eventually develop into seeds, topped with a style and a stigma to receive the pollen for fertilization.

In any individual flower, the stigmas are always ripe and ready for pollination before the anthers develop sufficiently to shed their own pollen. This increases the likelihood of flowers receiving pollen from a different plant – a useful evolutionary tool called cross pollination. After fertilization up to about eight seeds develop in each pod. Both in the wild and in gardens, hellebores hybridize frequently, which leads to the creation of intermediate plants. These cause confusion among both botanists and gardeners.

Flowering usually takes place in late winter and early spring. After this period, the stems tend to arch outwards from the plant as the seeds develop and become heavier. From late spring onwards, the pods split and the seeds drop out away from the crown of the plant. Each stem usually carries up to six or seven flowers in a head, or sometimes just one, especially in the case of *H. niger*. Each flower has a leafy bract behind it. In caulescent species – *H. argutifolius, H. lividus* and *H. foetidus* – there are far more flowers in a head.

The seeds are generally slightly kidney-shaped, about the size of mouse droppings, with a white ridge along one edge. This ridge contains fats and sugars, which attracts ants. These industrious insects distribute the seeds by carrying them away and storing them in crevices, hence the reason why hellebores are sometimes seen growing half way up a wall.

13

HELLEBORE CLASSIFICATION

The 16 wild species of the genus *Helleborus* are divided into six groups of species. These divisions are based on the following features in descending order of importance: obvious distinctions such as the presence of stems; whether or not the individual carpels are joined to one another at the base; the shape and surface texture of the pollen grains; the size and shape of the seeds; the capacity of plants to hybridize with each other; obvious and distinctive characteristics of the foliage; and flower colour.

As the flowers age and pods start to develop, the flowers of Helleborus foetidus flare, bringing a new character to the plant and extending its already long season.

Using these various distinctions, the genus is grouped into six sections as shown in the chart below. As well as the hybrids listed in the chart, there are also a number of other hybrids between species of different groups. This means that the boundaries between the six groups are not absolutely rigid, and in a few cases they break down. This is one of the puzzles that plant taxonomists are considering at present. Recent genetic research indicates that from a strictly botanical point of view these divisions may be even less clear cut but they remain very helpful to gardeners.

Botanical Groupings

Section	Species included
1 Helleborus	*H. niger*
2 Chenopus	*H. argutifolius, H. lividus* and their hybrid *H. × sternii*
3 Dicarpon	*H. thibetanus*; this species hybridizes with many other species
4 Griphopus	*H. foetidus*
5 Helleborastrum	*H. atrorubens, H. croaticus, H. cyclophyllus, H. dumetorum, H. multifidus, H. odorus, H. orientalis, H. purpurascens, H. torquatus* and *H. viridis*. Hybrids within this group are known as *H. hybridus*
6 Syncarpus	*H. vesicarius*

THE NAMING OF HELLEBORES

The few common names for hellebores are mainly well known: Christmas rose (*H. niger*) is known for its early flowering, although this is relatively rare; Lenten rose (*H. hybridus*) flowers regularly through Lent; the stinking hellebore (*H. foetidus*) has foliage that emits an unpleasant smell when bruised; and the British native *H. viridis* is often known as the green hellebore, although many other green-flowered species are now grown in gardens by enthusiasts.

The botanical naming of the wild species is relatively straightforward, although the confirmation of *H. croaticus* as a separate species is a relatively recent development. The naming of the cultivated forms, however, is altogether less clear and more confusing. The one entirely clear aspect of this is that only forms propagated vegetatively by division can be given cultivar names. Most hellebores sold in the trade and distributed among

This strongly coloured yellow form of Helleborus hybridus *has, for many years, been grown at Myddelton House, the garden of the famous plantsman E.A. Bowles.*

enthusiasts, however, are not propagated vegetatively; they are raised from seed. Since hellebore flowers are specifically adapted for cross pollination (see p.13), this leads to a number of problems.

Plants raised from seed from a named cultivar must not be given the same cultivar name because the offspring can be highly variable in appearance as a result of cross pollination. Many hellebores on sale that are raised from seed, however, are the result of carefully controlled pollination, sometimes by hand, to ensure that the resulting plants are uniform in terms of flower colour, foliage colour and habit or other features. These are sometimes known informally by colour, such as *H. hybridus* yellow, sometimes they are given group names, for example *H.* × *sternii* Blackthorn Group, sometimes they are called strains, like *H.* × *sternii* Bulmer's blush strain, and sometimes they are given cultivar names, such as *H.* × *sternii* 'Boughton Beauty' and *H. foetidus* 'Sienna'.

The problem in practice is that the designation of a particular form as a cultivar does not guarantee that plants fit a particular description. The seed from which they are raised may be the result of uncontrolled cross pollination, and so the resulting plants may be highly variable in appearance. By contrast, forms designated as a strain or group, or even named vaguely by colour, may fit a particular set of features far more consistently.

Botanists have agonized over this for many years and have come to no definite conclusion that is helpful to gardeners. As a result, unless you can be certain that a cultivar is propagated vegetatively by division or the seed is the result of controlled pollination, the best advice is to choose plants yourself, in the flesh, so to speak, when they are in flower.

How to grow Hellebores

Soils, siting and planting

Hellebores are neither difficult to raise nor difficult to grow. They are tough and resilient, but like all plants, they know what they like and they thrive more heartily if their tastes are met. Treat them thoughtfully and try to give them the conditions they require.

In general, hellebores prefer neutral or slightly alkaline (limy) soils; a pH of about 7.0 seems ideal, although good plants are often also seen around rhododendrons in gardens with acid soil conditions. Acid soil can be made more accommodating by liming the whole area before planting, using an alkaline organic material like spent mushroom compost when improving the soil, or by adding 1–2oz (25–50g) of lime (calcium carbonate) to the planting mix (see p.20) when planting individual hellebores. An annual top dressing of a similar amount of lime per plant, before mulching, can also help. And on very acid soils, even the rhododendrons will appreciate a little lime.

Recommendations for individual species are given later, but it is true, fortunately, that all types of soil can grow good hellebores, although they all hate waterlogged conditions. In severe cases, installing drainage channels can alleviate waterlogging and will also benefit most other plants. Organic matter and grit worked into the soil to improve the flow of water to lower levels can also be successful, and creating raised beds also works well. Planting near to mature trees, which naturally absorb a great deal of moisture from soggy soil, is a clever ecological solution for shade-loving hellebores.

A superb spotted pink form of Helleborus hybridus – not a named cultivar but an example of the high quality of modern seed strains.

18

As a rule, the more moisture the soil retains, the more sun and open exposure hellebores will tolerate. On heavy clay soils, which tend to be moisture retentive, most hellebores tolerate some sunshine, but the plants will still benefit from soil improvement. In sandy, well-drained soil, the plants appreciate more shade. The addition of generous amounts of organic matter greatly improves both the moisture-holding capacity and the nutrient levels of the soil.

Organic matter is the key, but the addition of coarse grit can also improve heavy soil. Thorough winter digging in the traditional style allows both grit and organic matter to be incorporated; forking these materials to the depth of two spade blades will create noticeable improvements to the workability of the soil and the health of the plants. Well-rotted garden compost or manure, leafmould, spent mushroom compost and bagged soil improvers from the garden centre are all suitable forms of organic matter.

Improving the soil is only part of the answer. Preparing thoroughly before planting is also very important. It pays to prepare well. Plants of *H. hybridus* in particular develop deep and extensive root systems, which allow them access to potential reserves of moisture and nutrients deep in the soil. Hellebores will remain in one site for many years, developing into large and impressive clumps; it is not necessary, indeed it is a mistake, to split the plants regularly as is usual with many other perennials. So planting time is the one opportunity to improve the soil at root level.

Dig out a hole to the depth of your spade and, if possible, 45cm (18in) across. Fork over the base of the hole and then work in some friable organic matter. The most generally available organic matter is old peat- or soil-based potting compost or the contents of old growing bags; anything is better than nothing. Add to this a long-term, slow-release fertilizer and some grit on poorly drained soils. Work at least half a bucket of this mix into the base of the hole, then tread firmly. If the general planting area has been hurriedly prepared or if organic matter could not be applied liberally over the area in general preparation, work some of the above planting mix into the soil that will be used to refill the hole.

The level of planting is important. Container-grown plants can simply be planted so that the surface of the compost in the container is level with the surrounding soil. Plants moved from elsewhere in the garden should be set so that the final soil level is 2.5cm (1in) above the point at which the roots are attached to the crown. Finally, refill the hole with soil, firm the ground carefully with the ball of your foot, level the soil off and water

Helleborus vesicarius has distinctive celery-like foliage and flowers unlike those of any other species.

the plant in well. I like to water the plants with a liquid feed the day before planting, adding some liquid feed to the can when watering in afterwards. Finish with a 5cm (2in) mulch of weed-free organic matter.

Plants of *H. hybridus* and many of the smaller species will stay undisturbed for many years, so thorough soil preparation is essential. Shorter-lived species, such as *H. argutifolius* and *H. foetidus*, will thrive on less preparation. *H. vesicarius* demands warm, sunny and well-drained conditions, while *H. lividus*, and to a lesser extent *H. × sternii*, are also different in that they require better drainage and more sunshine. See individual entries for further details (see the 'Choosing your Hellebores' section, pp.58–86).

Cultivation and aftercare

Relatively little attention is required during the year. An annual mulch of weed-free organic matter in autumn, perhaps mixed with bonemeal or another slow-release fertilizer, helps to conserve moisture in summer and provide a steady flow of nutrients. At the same time, and certainly before the end of the year, it pays to remove most of the old foliage of *H. hybridus* plants and of many other species; this is a precaution against the spread of black spot disease (see p.39). By the time the flower stems start to emerge, all the foliage should have been removed. Trim off the foliage of caulescent species towards the base of the stems as it begins to deteriorate and look tatty.

Check plant labels regularly, as blackbirds have a habit of flinging them around, and generous mulching can bury them and their text becomes illegible. After flowering, snip off the flower stems at the base when their colour has drained, unless seed is required. The caulescent species should have the whole flowering stem removed at the crown after flowering; new shoots will be seen emerging from the crown and these will provide the foliage and flowers for the coming season.

Growing hellebores in containers

Hellebores suit containers. Some species are best grown in these conditions, while others will take to them well. *H. lividus* and *H. vesicarius* are most conveniently grown in large pots; they can then be moved and given the necessary frost protection in autumn and winter, and then brought outside again in spring. *H.* × *ballardiae*, *H.* × *ericsmithii* and the smaller forms of *H.* × *sternii* also make excellent plants for pots. *H. hybridus* and other species are less successful as they produce very extensive root growth and are also susceptible to rotting if the crown remains wet after watering.

These plants not only look best in terracotta pots, but as terracotta allows moisture to evaporate through the sides, it helps prevent waterlogging. When preparing pots, remember that drainage is crucial. Crock the pots well and use a well-drained but rich potting compost, such as John Innes No. 3 with the addition of 25 per cent horticultural grit by volume. Top with 1cm (½in) of grit after potting. Water attentively

The indispensable Helleborus × sternii inherits the pewtery foliage colour and red tints from one parent, H. lividus, and the large green flowers and bold toothed leaves from the other, H. argutifolius.

during the growing season and feed regularly with a balanced liquid feed. Every year or two, remove the plant from its pot, scrape off some of the compost from the root ball and replace it with fresh material. After a few years in the same pot, move the plant to a larger container.

Propagation of hellebores

Hellebores can be propagated by division or by seed. Division is a vegetative process and all the resultant plants will be identical to the parent plant. In contrast, propagation by seed is a sexual process, and the offspring may be very similar – or they may not.

Hellebore seeds germinate readily, as can usually be seen simply by looking around mature plants in most gardens; the seedlings are often obvious. While it is indeed possible to let the seed drop and germinate, however, treating the seeds with a little more care will yield more flowering plants more quickly (see 'Raising Hellebores from Seed', pp.28–35).

'Ushba' is a superb white Helleborus hybridus *raised by Helen Ballard, which should be propagated by division and not seed to be sure of true stock.*

Division of most species, hybrids and cultivars is both straightforward and practical. But first a warning: do not simply detach pieces from the edge of your cherished clump and replant them elsewhere or give them away. The youngest and most vigorous growth is always at the edge of the clump, while the tired, woody and unproductive growth is at the centre. Removal of the most vigorous growth, leaving the tired old centre behind, weakens the original plant and it may cease flowering and fade away altogether.

There are two approaches to division: the simple approach, which is only modestly productive, and a more careful and thorough productive approach, which yields more plants. In both cases, the best time to divide the Lenten roses (*H. hybridus*) and also the hybrids with *H. niger,* such as *H.* × *nigercors* and *H.* × *ericsmithii,* is in late summer and early autumn, towards the end of August or in September in Britain. These hellebores initiate a burst of root growth in autumn and the optimum time to divide them is immediately prior to this spurt of root development. This allows newly divided plants to grow new roots and settle in immediately.

The Christmas rose (*H. niger*) and the many relatively demure species from the Balkans, such as *H. torquatus* and *H. atrorubens,* are best divided in early spring. Brave souls wishing to divide *H. vesicarius* should do so in autumn, but my advice is not to; a mature plant is so impressive it is best left alone, and the chances of establishing divisions are not good.

Not all hellebores can be propagated by division. Those in the caulescent group – *H. argutifolius,* *H. lividus,* *H.* × *sternii* and *H. foetidus* – can be divided in theory, but their tendency to a short life is usually exacerbated by the disruption caused by division. There are also practical problems associated with dividing deep-rooted plants with very compact rootstocks and such tall top-growth.

Simple division

Tie the foliage of the plant together loosely with string, then use a large digging fork to lift the plant. The root system is extensive, so try to remove as much root and soil as possible. Then untie the foliage and split the plant using the traditional 'two forks' technique. The root system of a mature plant is very woody, so you will need two stout digging forks. Borrow one from a neighbour, if necessary, rather than use a light border fork.

To split a clump using two forks, force one fork downwards vertically through the centre of the clump. You may need to put your weight on the fork to force it through or even hit the top of the tines with a mallet! Then force in a second fork back-to-back with the first. Push the handles apart, then together and keep working to split the plant. Watch your fingers. When it eventually breaks in two, assess the sizes of the resulting pieces. An old clump 30cm (12in) across or more can probably be split into four pieces by repeating the process on each of the first two halves. Smaller pieces can be left without dividing again. Write labels for each division at this point. Trim off any damaged leaves and replant at once. If you find the roots especially tough, use a sharp spade to slice through the tightly congested growth.

Productive division

The problem with simple division of hellebores is that they often miss one or two year's flowering. They also take a long time to recover and grow strongly again. So if a slow recovery is inevitable, why not make more than just a few plants?

Lift the plant as described for simple division, shake off as much soil as possible, then use a wheelbarrow to move the plant to an out-of-the way corner or near a drain. Next, use a garden hose to wash as much soil off the plant as possible. Put your finger over the end of the pipe or use an adjustable jet to generate plenty of pressure to remove stones and soil. If this is not practical, wash off the soil in an old galvanized bath, an old water tank or a large bucket.

When the soil is washed off the roots, the full root system will be revealed in detail. Use secateurs, an old bread knife or even a small, sharp spade to split it into a number of large pieces, discarding the oldest, woodiest part of the crown and retaining the younger growth. After tidying up, these large pieces can then be replanted. Alternatively, they can be further split into smaller sections, which is the most productive approach. Use secateurs to cut some of the older woody material away. Try to break the clump down into pieces with one or two leaves, a healthy pointed 'nose' (from which new top growth will come) and plenty of pale roots; the black roots are the older roots and will not re-grow. As each small piece

Use a sharp knife to detach divisions from the crown of a well-washed plant.

is separated, trim off any damaged foliage and any long black roots, then temporarily place each piece in moist potting compost or any other damp organic matter to prevent it drying out. You

This ideal division has plenty of young roots, two strong shoots and some older foliage.

will sometimes find seedlings growing in the centre of the clump; remember that they will not be identical to the clump that is being divided, so either discard them or label them separately.

Your chosen pieces can then either be planted out in a new site, planted in a nursery area for a year or two to develop, or potted up for planting once they have started to grow strongly. When planting out in their final flowering site, prepare the soil well (see p.18); if planting in a nursery area for a year, choose a partially shaded site with good soil and fork in plenty of weed-free organic matter into the top 30cm (12in) of soil, treading the soil well before planting out 23–30cm (9–12in) apart. Finally, water them in with a liquid feed and mulch with weed-free organic matter. Make sure the soil stays moist and give the divisions two or three further liquid feeds during spring.

You may prefer to pot up your new plants, which is the best option for smaller divisions, and it will be necessary if the splits are to be given away or taken to a plant sale. Use a well-drained, good-quality, soil-based potting compost, such as John Innes No. 3. The tall, deep pots known as rose pots or 'long toms' are ideal for larger divisions but can be hard to find; alternatively, large divisions can go in 16cm (6½in) pots, and the smallest can go in 9cm (3½in) pots.

Pot up divisions into individual pots for a good start before planting them in their final positions.

Keep the pots in a sheltered place outside, and be sure to sit them on a gravel bed so the compost drains well and does not become waterlogged. Another way is to site the pots in a cold frame with the lights, or lids, raised whenever the weather is anything but cold and snowy, or in a cold greenhouse. Make sure you ventilate a cold greenhouse thoroughly to keep the temperatures low on sunny days. Look out for aphids at this stage and deal with them accordingly (see p.39).

Some divisions may flower in the spring after dividing. The flower buds develop during summer, so when the plants are divided, the embryonic flower buds are already in place. However, to encourage the plants to settle more quickly and to flower productively in succeeding years, it pays to remove these first-year flowers as they start to develop.

Raising hellebores from seed

Try to sow hellebore seeds in midsummer, and no later than late summer. Although a few growers sow seed direct in the open ground, sowing in pots is altogether more dependable. The seeds need room to develop, and their young roots can be very vigorous, so use large pots – 13cm (5in) plastic pots are ideal – allowing room to space out the seeds.

Make sure the pot is clean, then fill it loosely with a soil-based seed compost, such as John Innes Seed Compost. Alternatively, if you habitually use a peat- or coir-based multipurpose compost, or any other particular compost for raising perennials from seed, then use that instead. Fill the pot loosely to just below the rim, tap it on the bench or table to settle the compost, and then firm *gently*. Firming too hard results in poor drainage and rotting seedlings. Ensure the compost is level.

The seeds are sufficiently large to be sown individually. A 13cm (5in) pot will take 21 seeds, evenly spaced. There is a lot to recommend sowing in a systematic manner. Evenly space a row of five seeds across the middle of the pot, then place another four seeds across the first row to make a cross. Next, place two seeds in each space between the arms of the cross, and finally place one seed in the middle of each quarter. A larger 16cm (6½in) pot will accomodate 30 seeds.

Never use the shallow, 13cm (5in) 'half pots', in which pot

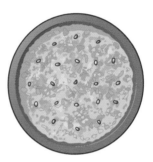

Space the seeds out carefully in the seed pot so that each seedling has space to develop.

chrysanthemums are sometimes sold, and never use a pot smaller than 10cm (4in), even if you only have a few seeds to sow. Neither pot provides sufficient root space. After sowing, cover the seeds with about 1cm (½in) of horticultural grit or pea gravel. The pots are then best stood on gravel or grit in a cold frame, then watered well.

A humid atmosphere encourages germination but in a summer cold frame this can be hard to create. A solution is to replace the glass light with a timber panel such as a piece of treated plywood or to pin a sheet of white reflective polythene to the frame for the summer to help keep the seeds from heating up and drying out. The seeds do not need to be kept in the dark, but a humid atmosphere is certainly helpful. An alternative is to cover each pot with an upturned terracotta saucer, or a plastic saucer kept in place with a stone. Each cover must be removed for watering, however, and then replaced, which is an irritating business.

One final task is to protect the seeds from disturbance and pests, especially from the attentions of hungry mice. Individual pot covers will do the job nicely, but a covering of chicken wire to screen the pots from investigating blackbirds and cats also works. The setting of mouse traps may also prove necessary.

Keep the seeds consistently moist, and inspect the pots every two or three days from mid-autumn onwards for signs of germination. As soon as the first seeds germinate, bring the pots into the light and remove their covers, but continue to protect them from mice. Ensure also that the seedlings are protected against slugs, which can easily eat a frame full of seedlings in a single night. Germination of fresh seed can be close to 100 per cent. Fresh seed of all species should germinate by the middle of winter, particularly that of *H. niger*, but sometimes before late autumn. Old seed, if it germinates at all, may come up at any time. Protection from severe winter weather is advisable when the forecast indicates such precautions. Watering should continue to be consistent, and protection against mice and slugs must be vigilant.

At this early stage the young seedlings are vulnerable to slugs so take precautions.

Germination and pricking out

Seedlings develop at different rates. Those of *H. hybridus* tend to be the most vigorous, and by early spring seedlings should be ready for pricking out. Those of the smaller, less vigorous species will be slower to reach the right stage, which is when the first true leaf is showing between the two simple seed leaves. The seedlings can be planted out into the open ground at this stage, but it is far preferable to prick them out into pots, which should be 9cm (3½) in size. Square 8cm (3in) pots are also used sometimes, but provide much less root space. Any good potting compost is suitable, although good quality John

Innes No. 1 is my first choice.

To prick out the seedlings, tip the root ball of the seed pot out on to a table or bench and carefully pull the roots apart until individual plants are separated. Never handle the vulnerable seedlings by their stem, which is easily damaged, but always hold them by a leaf. Pot up each seedling gently, ensuring that the roots are well spread out, with the final level of the potting compost just below the seed leaves. Firm gently, topping with 5mm (¼in) of horticultural grit if you have it, and water well. Make sure the seedlings are labelled and stand them in an open cold frame to grow on. By late spring, all the seedlings should have germinated and been pricked out.

As the first true leaves start to show their character, the seedlings are ready for pricking out.

There are a few slight exceptions to this advice. Seeds of the temperamental *H. vesicarius* should be spaced a little more widely in their seed pots, then left until early autumn of the year following sowing. Then, as the seedlings start into growth, prick them out into deep, 10cm (4in) pots for growing on. Some species, such as *H. argutifolius*, *H. foetidus*, *H. lividus*, *H. niger* and its hybrids, and *H. × sternii*, make large root systems unusually quickly and their seedlings benefit from pricking out into slightly larger pots.

Planting out or potting on

Seedlings may often grow rapidly, especially if encouraged with an occasional liquid feed, and when the roots start to appear through the drainage holes of the pot they are ready for planting out. Those seedlings in whose characteristics you have reason to have faith can be planted out in their final positions. Hellebores that develop large root systems, such as forms of *H. argutifolius*, *H. foetidus*, *H. niger* and *H. × sternii*, can also be planted out directly into their final positions, as long as you have no reason to believe they have been cross pollinated and you are sure of their final features. However, any species plants or forms of *H. hybridus* in which you have doubt as to their final features, are best assessed first. This can be managed either by potting on into larger pots or by planting in a nursery area until they first flower.

If potting on for assessment before planting, use tall, deep pots known as rose pots and the same potting compost as used when first pricking out. To ensure that the plants never go short of nutrients, either add a long-term, slow-release fertilizer to the compost, or be sure to feed regularly. If the protection of a cold greenhouse, polythene tunnel or cold frame is available, development will be more rapid than if the plants are stood in a sheltered place outside. Ensure that the plants do not dry out in these warmer, protected conditions.

Seedlings can also be set out in a well-prepared, partially shaded nursery area, and planted 30cm (12in) apart to grow on for assessment. Often the flowers that appear in the first flowering season may be different, and often inferior, to the flowers produced by the same plant in later years. For example, a plant carrying unremarkable small greenish flowers in its first year may produce far more attractive, elegant pure white flowers in following years but, unfortunately, it may not. A two-year assessment is always best, but it is usually acceptable to pick out especially good specimens in their first year and they will usually stay good; it is probably wise to keep unexpectedly poor seedlings from good parents for a second year if the space is available. After careful assessment, desirable plants can be dug up and planted in their final positions.

SOURCES OF HELLEBORE SEED

Hellebore seed is available from a number of sources, but there is one factor that determines the choice: hellebore seed is best sown when it is fresh, preferably within a month or two of ripening. Seed from plants in your own garden is, therefore, the most convenient and obvious choice. It should be collected from your own plants in late spring or early summer and sown promptly.

Specialist societies and seed exchanges will send out hellebore seed by post, and many take the need for freshness very seriously. Some are very specific about the origin of the

very seriously. Some are very specific about the origin of the seed, so it is clear exactly what you will receive, while others are more vague. In some lists the word 'ex' is used; for example, seed may be listed as ex 'Greencups'. Do not be misled; it simply means that the seed has been collected from the cultivar 'Greencups' but gives no indication, let alone guarantee, as to the other parent or the uniformity of the offspring. This can degenerate into an especially misleading practice if the 'ex' disappears from labels, and the plants masquerade under the name of a cultivar when, in fact, they bear it no resemblance. Commercial seed companies also sell hellebore seed, but this is rarely fresh. Unless given special treatment (see 'Germinating old hellebore seed', p.34), germination will be slow, sporadic and may be almost non-existent.

Collecting your own seed

The advantage of sowing seed from your own hellebores is that you are aware of the plant from which the seed has come and whether it has been pollinated by bees or by your own intervention. This is an important factor in assessing the potential quality of the resulting plants. The seeds usually ripen soon as their drying pods show the first evidence of a split along one edge, snip off the whole flower into an A5-sized paper envelope. Label the envelope carefully, and stand it in a warm dry place. Keep checking the remaining flowerheads. If seed drops to the ground below the plant, through an oversight or holiday, it can usually be carefully collected with a teaspoon in the few days after it has fallen, before ants start to distribute it. Before sowing, empty the paper envelope on to a sheet of white paper. Open any pods that are not fully split and shake out the seed. Finally, remove the old flower parts and other debris, and the seed is ready to sow.

Germinating old hellebore seed

Sometimes only old seeds are available, and seeds from large commercial seed companies that arrive six months after harvest is, in the case of hellebores, classified as old. It is a waste to treat these seeds in the same way as fresh seed.

A mistaken belief is that hellebore seeds require a period of frost before they will germinate. In truth, what they need is a warm and moist period, followed by declining temperatures, after which germination takes place. A long period of cold is not required. The warm, moist period is provided by sowing the seed in summer and keeping it from drying out; then, as temperatures reduce naturally, germination is initiated.

If seeds are sown in winter, they receive the right treatment, but in the wrong order: cold first and warmth later in spring. So with old seeds, there are two ways of giving them the right sequence of conditions. The first is simply to keep the seeds, dry but refrigerated, until summer and sow them at the same time as fresh seed. The second method is to sow the seeds in winter, not later than midwinter (early January in the UK), but instead of standing the pots in a cold frame, put them in a propagator with the thermostat set at about 15°C (59°F), in a warm greenhouse, or on a bedroom windowsill – anywhere that will keep the seeds warm. After six weeks, move the pots outside where the seeds should germinate after a period of cold weather. Expect the germination of old seed, sown using the second method, to be about 50 per cent. Germination of old seed sown outside in winter is more often minimal and sporadic.

Self-sown seedlings

Ants often carry hellebore seeds to unexpected places, hence this plant of the stinking hellebore, Helleborus foetidus, *growing in a crevice in a limestone wall.*

Hellebores can be left to self sow, which they often do prolifically. This has one advantage, and a number of disadvantages. The advantage is that it involves the minimal amount of effort for the gardener, which for some is very significant. The disadvantages, however, outweigh this simple benefit.

First of all, some seeds are lost as ants move them to inhospitable sites and other creatures eat them. Germinating seeds are also easily damaged by routine cultivations

– a generous autumn mulch, for example, which smothers them very successfully. It is also much less easy to keep track of which seedlings came from which plant, especially if a group of different varieties are grown together. And sometimes seeds will fall into the middle of an established clump and germinate there. These will likely be missed and, more seriously, when the parent plant is propagated by division, seedlings may be split with the rest of the clump and be assumed to be identical, which they will not be.

In spite of these drawbacks, however, collecting and growing self-sown seedlings is an easy and productive way of making more hellebores. In spring, lift them carefully with a handfork and either plant them out in rows in a nursery area to grow on, or pot them up as described for seedlings raised in pots (see p.30). Be aware that unless the seeds are the result of careful hand pollination, they are unlikely to be identical to either of their parents.

Micropropagation of hellebores

The laboratory propagation of hellebores by tissue culture has been the focus of trials by a number of companies over many years. As with many other members of the buttercup family, such as delphiniums, the results with hellebores have been so far disappointing and expensive. In time, it is probable that the technical problems will be solved, but at present we must depend on traditional methods of production.

BREEDING HELLEBORES

There are two reasons why gardeners should take a hand in breeding their own hellebores. Firstly, by intervening before the bees carry out their rather arbitrary pollination, it is possible to be a great deal more certain about the colour and other characteristics of subsequent plants raised from your own seed. Secondly, there is always the chance of raising something genuinely new and interesting.

Fortunately, hellebore flowers are large and easy to work with. To pollinate them, start with a flower whose petals are about to open. At this stage, the stigma will be receptive to pollen, its own pollen will not be ripe and the flower will not be sufficiently open to be accessible to bees. Next, find an open flower whose pollen is ready; look closely and the pollen appears yellow and fluffy. Use a pair of tweezers to pull off a couple of stamens, then dust their pollen on to the stigma of the flower that will carry the seed. Label the flower and collect its seeds in summer, sowing in the usual way.

Flowers can be hand pollinated by dabbing the stigmas with stamens held in tweezers.

If manual pollination is not done in a timely manner, however, you must parcel up the flowers in muslin or fine net bags to prevent the bees from pollinating the flowers before you do. One major drawback of breeding hellebores is that it takes three years from pollination to the first flowering of the seedlings; not everyone has the patience.

This reliable all season plant, Helleborus × ericsmithii, has three different species in its parentage – H. niger, H. lividus and H. argutifolius.

PESTS AND DISEASES

Hellebores are relatively trouble-free when it comes to pests and diseases, but it always pays to be aware of the following possible problems.

Aphids

A wide range of different aphids attack hellebores, including a hellebore-specific aphid. They can be found inside the flower, which is often the first infestation of spring, and on new and under old leaves. The first sign of infestation may be a patchy glossiness to the foliage – honeydew – and a few empty white cast skins. Honeydew is dripped down from aphids feeding on the flowers and foliage above. Seedlings are also sometimes infested and growth may be slowed down as a result. Aphids also transmit virus diseases. Contact sprays based on fatty acids, rape seed oil or bifenthrin are effective but need careful application. There are currently no systemic insecticides available to amateur gardeners for use on outdoor plants, except those being grown in containers. Open flowers should not be sprayed or bees may be harmed.

Black death

This is a relatively recent, slightly mysterious, but highly destructive disease that shows as black foliage blotches bounded by leaf veins or by the veins in bracts. Black streaks may also be seen in flowers. Affected plants become stunted and distorted, and they often die. A virus is the most likely culprit, in which case it is a wise precaution to keep aphids under control. It may also be spread on secateurs. The only safe remedy is to dig up and burn infected plants. This disease is more common in large collections and in nurseries than in gardens.

Black spot

Black spot is the most widespread and destructive disease of hellebores as it attacks the flowers and stems as well as the foliage.

This is the most frequent and damaging of the diseases that infect hellebores. Black or brown blotches appear on the foliage, merging to create dead areas on the leaves. Other parts of the plant turn yellow and much of the foliage and flowers may be damaged. Flowers can be devastated and a year's display completely ruined. If the disease is present on the foliage, it is transferred to the emerging flower shoots as they grow through the leaves in winter. In some cases, flower buds may rot and the flower stems collapse.

Black spot affects the taller caulescent species in a slightly different way. Often, it attacks the flowering stems at the base during the winter and the stems rot before they can mature. Lesions may sometimes also appear higher on the stems, and the upper foliage can also be damaged. Most of the damage is caused by fungal infection, but bacterial infection is sometimes also involved.

It is always more prevalent in warm, wet conditions. Removal of much of the foliage of *H. hybridus* and similar species in autumn greatly reduces the chances of infection of the flowers and the carry over of disease. There are currently no fungicides available to amateur gardeners to control this disease.

Cut the old foliage from plants of Helleborus hybridus *in autumn to prevent the carry-over of black spot.*

Damping off

Seedlings rot off at soil level and collapse. This is caused by a variety of soil-borne fungi, usually as a result of re-using old seed compost or from watering with water from a rain butt. Badly compacted, waterlogged potting compost, poor drainage under seed pots, or physical damage to the seedlings during pricking out are other causes. Avoid all these potential mistakes. Water with a copper fungicide at the first sign of trouble.

Leaf and bud eelworm

A microscopic pest that lives within the leaves, causing brown or black areas sharply defined by the larger leaf veins. Symptoms are most likely to be seen from late summer to autumn. No chemical controls are available, so the damage has to be tolerated or the plants destroyed.

Leaf miner

A fly that attacks *H. foetidus* only. It was first recorded in Britain in 2000 but is widely distributed, especially in southeast England. Brown leaf mines develop during autumn to winter, spoiling the appearance of the old foliage. Fortunately, the plants seem able to tolerate the damage. Removal of old foliage in winter stops the larvae from completing their development.

Mice

Mice can be troublesome in two ways: they can eat hundreds of seedlings in a single night and they also eat the buds and flowers of mature plants. They often leave distinctive, neat piles of debris at the base of the plants. Traps, or perhaps a predatory cat, are the answer.

Slugs and snails

Cutting away almost all the foliage in the autumn before the buds emerge ensures that black spot disease does not attack the new season's flowers.

These pests have two modes of attack: they devour seedlings growing in their pots, and they can also climb plants and eat the buds and stamens. Slugs and snails are sometimes seen inside the pendulous flowers of *H. hybridus* in wet spells, but flower damage is rarely extensive. To protect seedlings, cover the seeds with sharp grit and then a pot cover. Slug pellets and other control methods should be in place alongside the seed pots from the first.

Smut

An uncommon disease but sometimes seen in large collections. The leaf or flower stems split vertically to reveal black, dust-like spores. There is no treatment other than to carefully cut off and burn infected parts of plants.

Vine weevil

Increasingly common in many garden situations, mature garden plants usually tolerate infestation without revealing symptoms, although vigour may also be disappointing. Vine weevil can be troublesome, however, when plants are grown in pots for extended periods. The grubs eat roots and are not visible above the soil. Symptoms include poor growth, and the top-growth may seem poorly anchored and may eventually break away when the grubs have eaten through the roots. Biological control with the pathogenic nematode *Heterohabditis megidis* is effective in late summer, as are insecticides containing imidacloprid.

Vine weevil is an increasingly common problem; the adults sometimes chew the edges of the foliage while the more damaging white grubs feed on the roots.

Virus

Apart from black death (see p.39), the occasional virus symptoms seen are pale mottling patterns on the leaves and unusually shiny, stiff and jaggedly toothed foliage combined with a general loss of vigour. Dig up and burn affected plants. Older named clones propagated by division are especially likely to be infected by virus. Although clear physical symptoms may not be obvious, weak growth, unusually slow expansion of clumps and slowness of new divisions to develop into healthy new plants are all signs of virus infection.

HELLEBORES IN THE GARDEN

Hellebores are an essential element of the winter and spring garden. Their wide colour range, their tolerance of icy winter weather and the general resilience of most forms allows almost all to be grown without special care and attention in most soils usually encountered by gardeners. They are ideal for woodland gardens, a few grow well in Mediterranean plantings, and there is a place for hellebores in border displays throughout the garden. Some types are particularly suited to containers.

WINTER GARDENS

For many gardeners, hellebores will always be an integral part of a winter corner or, in a larger space, a complete winter garden. In combination with shrubs, bulbs, and evergreen and early-flowering perennials, it is not difficult to create colour with hellebores all through winter.

The background of a winter garden can comprise deciduous and evergreen shrubs. Deciduous shrubs with colourful winter stems, like the red-stemmed *Cornus alba* 'Sibirica', which is good with *Helleborus odorus*, and the yellow-stemmed *Salix alba* subsp. *vitellina*, which is good with *Helleborus foetidus* Wester Flisk Group, can be part of the background. Under a pale and sharply coloured witch hazel, such as *Hamamelis* × *intermedia* 'Pallida', a plum-purple-flowered *Helleborus hybridus* is ideal.

The neat and prolific evergreen shrub *Viburnum tinus* 'Gwenllian', with pink buds opening to white flowers, makes a fine background for a white-flowered *Helleborus hybridus*, while

This sparkling winter combination features two plants with attractions in other seasons; the scarlet berries of Iris foetidissima follow dusky mauve summer flowers, while the bright green saucers of Helleborus argutifolius are accompanied by bold year-round foliage.

a white-variegated evergreen euonymus, like *Euonymus japonicus* 'Latifolius Albomarginatus', will set off a red-flowered *Helleborus hybridus* well. Other pretty companions will be clumps of snowdrops (*Galanthus*), which also look good in front of deciduous shrubs with colourful winter stems, along with *Crocus chrysanthus*. Pulmonarias and epimediums, whose foliage makes great ground cover, also associate well.

On acid soils, rhododendrons and pieris provide shelter, which most hellebores may not actually need, but will certainly appreciate. White-flowered *H. hybridus* often stands up to the weather least well; a battering from icy wind damages the fragile petals and bracts allowing black spot to infect. Shelter helps prevent this, and a cosy dappled corner, with evergreen foliage in the background to set off the flowers well, is an ideal place in which to develop a large clump.

THE WOODLAND TAPESTRY

Both the flamboyant *Helleborus hybridus* and its forms, and the more demure species like *H. dumetorum* and *H. viridis* are perhaps at their best in a tapestry of winter and spring flowers and foliage plants. Backed by daphnes, pieris, smaller-flowered rhododendrons like Bluebird Group and 'Yellow Hammer', and scented evergreens like *Sarcococca confusa*, the Party Dress hybrids, the *H. hybridus* forms in their many colours, the green-flowered species and double forms of *Helleborus torquatus* can all be interplanted with a wide variety of choice woodland perennials and bulbs.

Allowing hellebores to self sow results in a forest of dramatically variable seedlings; if this suits you, the outcome will be delightful but unpredictable. With self-sown *Crocus speciosus*, *C. tommasinianus* and *Cyclamen coum* forms, plus clumps of choice snowdrops (*Galanthus*), which may also self sow, and wood anemones (*Anemone nemorosa*) meandering through it all, the result will be a captivating, changing pattern of colour and texture.

The hellebores can also be kept in discreet clumps, as can the snowdrops and named crocuses. If the whole planting is more intensively managed, plants and clumps of different sizes can be established in a flow of integrated cultivars so it all looks as if it

In a naturalistic wild garden setting, snowflakes, Leucojum vernum, and hellebores mingle together to create delightful winter and spring pictures.

is evolving naturally, but is in fact thoughtfully planned. Other plants that are useful in these settings, and appreciate the care and attention, include scillas, cardamines, trilliums, dog's-tooth violets (*Erythronium*), pale-yellow-flowered *Anemone* × *lipsiensis* 'Pallida', special primroses, unusual forms of *Iris foetidissima* with white or straw-coloured winter berries, plus hardy *Adiantum* species and other small ferns.

To cater for slow-growing species hellebores, it often pays to create raised beds. These should be no more than 30cm (12in) high, although 15cm (6in) is often enough to allow improved drainage on heavy soils or increased water retention on sandy soils. Working in as much leafmould or garden compost as possible works wonders. Raised to a more convenient working level, the plants can be looked after closely, tended carefully and their neighbours managed to ensure a balance of growth.

Clumps of this double white primrose, Primula vulgaris 'Alba Plena' are planted just far enough away from the dense foliage of the vigorous white Helleborus hybridus to avoid being smothered but close enough to create an attractive association.

Mediterranean plantings

A few hellebore species are at their best in informal, Mediterranean-style plantings. Dry and sunny in summer, and moist and sheltered in winter, a structure of evergreen cistus, phlomis, rosemaries, shrubby salvias and euphorbias, plus brooms (*Cytisus*) can make a structure into which *Helleborus argutifolius* and all the forms of *H.* × *sternii* can be integrated. Mulch with grit or gravel to make an attractive background and to suit more demanding plants. The smaller *H.* × *sternii* forms, Ashwood strain and Blackthorn Group, with their neat habit and silvered foliage, are splendid in front of pink-flowered *Cistus creticus* or *C.* 'Silver Pink' and among self-sown *Muscari latifolium* or crocuses.

When allowed to make bold specimens, *Helleborus argutifolius* and the equally tall, but red-tinted *H.* × *sternii* 'Boughton Beauty' can be truly impressive, especially when discreetly supported using a slim bamboo cane carefully positioned behind the stem and tied with green sisal twine. With figs and vines, these hellebores set the visual tone of a Mediterranean summer, and they can also host a lightweight annual climber like the orange-and-yellow-flowered *Lathyrus belinensis* or the red-and-white-flowered *L. clymenum articulatus*. Make sure that a bushy shrub, such as one of the small cistuses, is set in front to mask their bare basal stems.

The mixed border

Hellebores can make an important contribution to a mixed border, and many are tough enough to take the rough and tumble, such as *Helleborus hybridus*, *H. argutifolius* and some forms of *H.* × *sternii*. Set at the front, perhaps with an evergreen shrub as shelter to the shady side, a good-quality form of *H. hybridus* with species crocuses and snowdrops (*Galanthus*) naturalized around makes quite a feature. Later, the bold foliage of hellebores looks well with narrow, grassier leaves for contrast: silver-blue *Elymus magellanicus* striking through the bold and deep green hellebore leaves is ideal. Large, but still narrow foliage also works well. *Iris* 'Holden Clough', with its intriguing mustard-and-brown flowers, also demands a front-of-the-border spot, and its upright foliage contrasts well with

hellebores as do kniphofias and *Sisyrinchium striatum*. If the soil is moisture retentive, the hellebores will be happy in the sun that these plants require.

Further back in the border, *Helleborus argutifolius* and *H.* × *sternii* 'Boughton Beauty' look dramatic in front of a tiered viburnum, like *V. plicatum* 'Mariesii' and with slender *Iris sibirica* foliage. A climbing dicentra or its biennial relative *Adlumia fungosa* can use the hellebore for support. Both these hellebore species also make a distinctive contribution in winter before they even open their flowers. Their bold leaf structures, picked out in white frost on a bright morning, make a most dramatic feature in a mixed border.

WILD GARDENS

In shady wild gardens, *Helleborus foetidus* comes into its own. Set out a few plants of any cultivar, except the yellow-leaved forms which are less vigorous, with ferns, bluebells (*Hyacinthoides*) and *Carex pendula*, and they will soon be self sowing. The relatively

Helleborus foetidus 'Wester Flisk' emerges through an intricate mass of the bronze Carex comans; both are evergreen so create an all season combination ideal in smaller gardens.

A skimmia in bud backs a deep dusky purple form of Helleborus hybridus *with the vigorous snowdrop* Galanthus 'Atkinsii' *alongside and a self sown seedling of* H. foetidus *adding blue-tinted green foliage to this varied plant picture.*

short lifespan of *H. foetidus* plants ensures that no one specimen ever becomes over dominant. As seedlings germinate and become established, older specimens fade away leading to a slowly but constantly changing woodland picture. The plants are also tough enough to take the shade and the competition, even from ivy running across the ground. They need almost no care, just cut out the old stems after flowering. They also look superb in the frost on winter mornings.

THE HERBACEOUS BORDER

The traditional herbaceous border is not really the place for *Helleborus hybridus* or the many green- or purple-flowered species. Most herbaceous borders are summer-flowering, so when hellebores flower in winter and early spring, the border is very bare. At this time, the summer perennials have been cut down and the hellebores have no background planting against which to show up and no companions with which to create a pleasing association; there is just bare soil. The lower levels of

a herbaceous border, however, are shady places in summer when taller perennials like phloxes and delphiniums are at their peak. This shade is useful for those hellebores that do not enjoy summer sun. While many are far too timid in stature and quiet in colouring for such empty spaces, *H. foetidus* is ideal.

Mature plants of any *H. foetidus* cultivar make boldly sculpted and impressive specimens, which display well among the short twigs of cut-down perennials in winter and early spring, especially if there is an evergreen or beech hedge as background. *H. foetidus* Wester Flisk Group, with its red colouring, and the large *H. foetidus* 'Green Giant' and 'Tros os Montes' are especially suitable. Three seedlings of these hellebores planted in a triangle soon make a bold planting in summer, if discreetly supported with a slim bamboo cane. They can be host to a lightweight, scrambling perennial climber like the lilac-flowered *Aconitum hemsleyanum*.

Even as the flowers of Helleborus foetidus *begin to turn to seed, a well grown plant is still a dramatic eye-catcher.*

The ground breaking hellebore breeder Helen Ballard created a very impressive shady border planted almost entirely with Helleborus hybridus *in a wide variety of colours.*

THE HELLEBORE BORDER

The well-known hellebore breeder Helen Ballard was famous for a long narrow border on the north side of her house, which was filled with mature plants of *Helleborus hybridus* in many colours. The soil was heavy and the garden cold, and they looked wonderful. If you have the space, this is a great idea, although thorough soil preparation is vital (see 'Soils, siting and planting', p.18), and the seedheads are best removed to prevent chaotic overcrowding. In winter and spring, the result is stunning.

Other plants can be added for variety. Helen Ballard had forms of *Cyclamen hederifolium* for their foliage as much as for their autumn and winter flowers, as well as specimen clumps of species peonies for the summer months. Keeping the planting simple, however, allows for time-saving blanket treatments – all the foliage can be cut off at once in autumn, the whole bed can be mulched in one go afterwards, and the whole bed dead-headed in a single session in late spring.

GROUNDCOVER

Some hellebores make good groundcover. These are types that produce broad, dense foliage on low plants, principally *Helleborus hybridus* forms. Their use as groundcover can be approached in two ways. The first method is to plant carefully selected, superior flowering size forms evenly over the area requiring cover. The second approach is to be less precious about the whole thing and simply plant seedlings from your best plants and let them get on with smothering the weeds with the minimum of attention.

For the first approach, prepare the soil thoroughly, much as if a hellebore bed was being planned. Choose plants of flowering size to ensure speedy and complete foliage cover. If seedheads are removed, the purity of the planting will be retained, leaf cover will develop strongly, and the continuance of separate clumps will allow for easy mulching and weeding. If seeds are allowed to fall, a forest of seedlings and young plants will develop. These may suppress the weeds well at first, but they will prove increasingly unpredictable in their colour and quality.

CHOOSING HELLEBORES

Attributes	
Bold foliage	When growing well, the foliage of *H. hybridus* is is often impressive; in summer *H.* × *sternii* 'Boughton Beauty' also has great impact.
Lacy foliage	*H. multifidus* subsp. *hercegovinus* has leaves prettily divided into many slender filaments, but is slow to establish; *H. foetidus* 'Green Giant' has narrowly fingered foliage.
Silver foliage	*H.* × *sternii* Ashwood strain is a dwarf form with prettily veined, silver leaves.
Variegated foliage	*H. argutifolius* 'Pacific Frost' is densely white-speckled, especially on young foliage; the occasional variegated forms of *H. hybridus* that appear have usually been poor things.
Red-tinted foliage	*H. lividus* is a strong reddish pink at its best, but the plant is not universally hardy; *H. foetidus* Wester Flisk Group has red-tinted stems, but it is variable.

Overall impact	*H. argutifolius* is tall, large-leaved and prolific; *H. foetidus* 'Green Giant' is the tallest of all, and a mature specimen is very impressive; *H. hybridus* is a good, pure white, single-flowered species – a real eye-catcher.
Most reliable for Christmas	*H. orientalis* subsp. *abchasicus* Early Purple Group is often in full flower at Christmas.
Fragrant flowers	*H. odorus* should be sniffed before you buy to be sure; *H. foetidus* 'Miss Jekyll' can be very sweet – sniff, then buy.
Easiest in full sun	*H. × sternii* and all its forms enjoy plenty of sunshine.
Easiest in deep shade	*H. foetidus* and all its forms are happy in shade, and they will even take dry shade.
Best in alpine house	*H. lividus* is a wonderful, neat and easy, all-season foliage plant with beautiful flowers.
Best talking point	*H. vesicarius* features 8cm (3in) seed pods, which look like balloons.
Best all-year-round	*H. × sternii* Blackthorn Group has good evergreen foliage, good flowers and is easy to grow.
Most often disappointing	*H. niger* needs thoughtful cultivation or it just fades away; *H. hybridus* mixed is unpredictable, often not mixed or with poor colours and the flower shapes are often poor too.
The hellebore for idiots	*H. × nigercors* is the one you can just plant and forget.

HELLEBORES IN POTS

While growing some hellebores in pots is the most convenient way to give them the conditions they require (see 'Growing hellebores in containers', p.22), some species, particularly *H. × sternii*, simply look good in containers. The recently introduced, dwarf, silvered forms of *H. × sternii* – Ashwood strain and Blackthorn Group – make excellent container plants. They can be used as specimens in individual containers and set on a sunny patio during winter and spring. Alternatively, they can be used as part of a winter and spring mixed planting with winter conifers, skimmias and clumps of dwarf bulbs in a large container of 45cm (18in) or more.

The misty pink and pale green flowers of Helleborus × sternii *Blackthorn Group top neat silvery foliage on compact plants, making it an ideal plant for all-year containers.*

The variegated cultivars of *Helleborus argutifolius* – 'Pacific Frost' and 'Janet Starnes' – also make good container plants. So much less tall than the more familiar green-leaved form, they require careful prevention of black spot (see 'Pests and Diseases', p.39). They can be used as specimens in individual containers, although the base of their stems may be rather bare by planting time. Another approach is to plant them in a mixed display in the same way as the dwarf *H.* × *sternii* forms; a neat, red-leaved bergenia like *B.* 'Wintermärchen' is an ideal companion.

HELLEBORES IN THE HOUSE

Have you ever wondered why you never see hellebores at the florist? Go into the garden next winter or spring, cut a stem from your favourite hellebore and bring it inside, then stand it in a vase of water. Within hours the flowers will be hanging over the side. So is there no way in which hellebore flowers can be treated to ensure that they perform better indoors? There are two problems: the tendency of the stems to be too weak to support the heads and the fragility of the flowers themselves.

A number of solutions have been suggested to help keep the stems rigid. They can be plunged up to their necks in warm water, the moment they are cut in the garden, and some gardeners report success from re-cutting the ends of the stem under water immediately after cutting. Another suggestion is to treat them as for tulips; make a hole with a pin through the top of each stem, below the flower. In my experience, none of these methods seems altogether reliable, but it does seem to be true that older stems stand up more effectively. If these are cut when the flowers are past their best and going to seed, therefore, and the petals stiffer and papery, the stems and fragile flowers seem to hold up better. After cutting, try not to give them too much of a shock by bringing them straight from a chilly garden into a warm room. Cut and place them in water at once, then bring them into a cool room and recut the stems under water before arranging them. Make sure you add flower food to the water.

Helleborus hybridus and the other species of this type seem the least successful. However, *H. foetidus* is sold as a cut flower on rare occasions, so if you have plenty to spare and can cut a few without ruining the garden display, the flowers of this species hold up better than most. A couple of other species last in water, for a few days anyway. *H.* × *nigercors* and *H.* × *ericsmithii*, although their stems are relatively short, inherit a degree of natural woodiness from *H. argutifolius*, which ensures that the stems remain upright in a vase. As the stems are undeniably short, however, they are best used in low table arrangements combined with berries of *Iris foetidissima* and the blue foliage of *Chamaecyparis pisifera* 'Boulevard' or a blue-leaved juniper.

The best way to enjoy the many colours of *H. hybridus* indoors is to float individual flowers on water or arrange them on damp moss. Nip off flowers with your fingers, or with a pair of sharp kitchen scissors, and lay them in a plastic food box while you collect more. Take them indoors and fill an elegant bowl with water and simply float the flowers on their backs. If you have access to fresh moss, partially fill a bowl with water, then fill it with fresh green moss and arrange the flowers on its surface. Such an arrangement makes a great centrepiece.

Choosing your hellebores

A very wide range of hellebores is available from nurseries, including all the hellebore species, and many can also be obtained from specialist seed companies. A great number of hellebores are sold simply by colour and without cultivar names, and many are only available from a single nursery so gardeners may have difficulty finding some of the named forms. Cultivars developed in the USA are rarely available in the UK and vice versa. Transatlantic plant purchasing is generally not possible for home gardens, although there is no restriction on the exchange of hellebore seeds.

Most hellebores are hardy in all areas of the UK, but where protection is required this is discussed in the relevant entry. Some plants are not hardy in the whole of the USA, with its extremes of climate, be it winter cold or summer heat (or both!), so the hardiness zone ratings are given as a guide to areas in which individual species will thrive. The lower the number, the colder the conditions the plant will tolerate. Most of the UK could be described as being in US zone 8.

In this chapter, all the hellebore species are described (although some are hardly grown in gardens) along with those cultivated forms listed in the *RHS Plant Finder*, which are well established in nurseries. Some North American cultivars are listed, plus some I think will become more widely available in the next few years.

Helleborus argutifolius (syn. *H. corsicus*)

The Corsican hellebore is a tall, easy and impressive, evergreen, sun-loving species with dramatic foliage and bright green

The attractive foliage of Helleborus argutifolius 'Pacific Frost'.

flowers. It belongs in the caulescent group and each year an increasing number of stems surge from a slowly spreading rootstock. The stems carry bold, evergreen leathery foliage, each leaf divided into three spiny leaflets, and from midwinter to mid-spring, depending on the season, the stems are topped with up to 30 green flowers, each 2.5–5cm (1–2in) across; their shape varies from prettily cupped to gappy with narrow petals. *H. argutifolius* grows naturally in Corsica. In gardens, it hybridizes readily with *H. lividus* to create the variable *H. × sternii*. Plant in good, preferably well-drained soil in a sunny situation. When growing well and in flower, the stems may need support from bamboo canes. Snip off the lower leaves as they begin to look tatty, and cut out the flowering stems at the base after flowering or seeding. The plant often declines after four or five years, but it self-sows readily. It is good in Mediterranean-style dry gardens with *Euphorbia characias* cultivars, and in winter gardens with coloured-stemmed dogwood (*Cornus*) and willow (*Salix*) cultivars. It can also be

The crowded green flower heads of Helleborus argutifolius *fall forward around the white flower heads of the invaluable evergreen* Viburnum tinus - *two fine winter essentials together.*

planted at the edge of a sunny, well-raised bed from where it will tumble down dramatically. Propagation is generally by seed only.

Height and spread: 1.2m (4ft)

Planting distance: 60–120cm (2–4ft)

Hardiness zones: 6–9

'**Little Erbert**' is a dwarf form reaching only 38cm (15in) in height.

'**Janet Starnes**' has gold- or yellow-speckled foliage, which is especially dense on young leaves, and the shoot tips are tinted pink. It is 60cm (24in) tall and rather variable.

'**Pacific Frost**' has cream- or white-speckled foliage, sometimes very densely marked, and the shoot tips are tinted red. It is 60cm (24in) tall and rather variable. It may not be genuinely distinct from 'Janet Starnes'.

Select strain is a North American strain with large, much darker, almost blue foliage, and a characteristic red blotch at the base of each leaf where it joins the stem. Many of the stems have red to purple stippling. It is 60–120cm (2–4ft) tall.

'**Silver Lace**' has pewtery green foliage, but it is not lacy. It has gappy flowers.

Helleborus atrorubens

This is a pretty, dainty species for partial shade. It is described as an enthusiasts' plant because it is not showy and is more difficult to grow than most. The deciduous foliage may be purple-tinted when young and is split into seven to nine main divisions; the outer divisions themselves are subdivided into about 10–15 elliptical divisions. In late winter and early spring, the noticeably open and branched flowering heads carry small, outward-facing flowers. These are rarely more than 5cm (2in) across, in green with purple backs, although sometimes they are all green, all purple or in various combinations. This is a variable species, both in flower colour and pattern, and in leaf shape. It grows wild in a small area of southeastern Slovenia and neighbouring Croatia and is not to be confused with *H. orientalis* subsp. *abchasicus* Early Purple Group, once widely known as 'Atrorubens'. *H. atrorubens* is best in a well-drained, leafy soil in the dappled shade of tall deciduous trees, or in other partially shaded situations. It seems especially prone to slug damage and its slender stems can be broken by gales. Demure partners like snowdrops (*Galanthus*), small primulas or asarums are ideal companions. Propagate by division as hybridizing with other hellebore species is likely.

Height and spread: 30–35cm (12–14in)
Planting distance: 30cm (12in)
Hardiness zones: 6–8

Combining the rather different qualities of Helleborus niger *and* H. lividus, *this pink-tinged, white-flowered plant,* H. × ballardiae, *is rather variable and sometimes features just four petals.*

Helleborus × ballardiae

This apparently unlikely hybrid combines the qualities of both its parents and is a very attractive, slightly tender plant for sunny borders or the cold greenhouse. The foliage is similar to that of *H. niger*, with up to eight divisions, but with a silvery sheen and pale veins. From early winter to mid-spring, short stems carry three or four flowers, which are usually pinkish green on the outside and a pale creamy green with pink tones on the inside, but the colouring can combine these three shades in varying degrees, with soft stripes sometimes seen. Flowers with four petals seem unusually frequent. The parents of this garden hybrid are *H. niger* and *H. lividus*, and it was formerly known as

'*H.* × *nigriliv*'. It inherits some lack of hardiness from *H. lividus*, but thrives outside in well-drained containers and sunny, sheltered, well-drained borders in relatively warm areas like the south of England. It is also excellent as a cold greenhouse and alpine house plant, where it can look superb. *H.* × *ballardiae* is unusually prone to black spot so keep the foliage dry when watering. Propagate by division as the plants are sterile.

Height: 30–35cm (12–14in); Spread 45cm (18in)
Planting distance: 38cm (15in)
Hardiness zones: 8–9

Helleborus croaticus

This deciduous plant has rounded foliage split into as many as 80 rather linear leaflets, and is generally similar to *H. atrorubens*. In midwinter to early spring, the flowers, which are reminiscent of *H. torquatus*, are carried in a rather open head with long, slender bracts and are usually dark purple, sometimes with reddish tints, inside and out. It grows wild in north-eastern Croatia. In the garden, it enjoys full sun, if supplied with sufficient moisture, but do not allow the soil to become waterlogged. This is a rarely seen, newly confirmed species, close to both *H. atrorubens* and *H. torquatus*. Propagate by division as hybridizing with other species is likely.

Height and spread: 38cm (15in)
Planting distance: 30cm (12in)
Hardiness zones: 6–8

Helleborus cyclophyllus

A vigorous, bold and impressive green-flowered hellebore that makes an imposing plant. The deciduous foliage is prettily silvered in fine hairs as it emerges and matures to a seven-segment leaf; the outer leaves repeatedly split to give about 25 oval divisions in all. The flowers appear up to seven per stem, from midwinter to early spring, about 5cm (2in) across, sometimes more. They are bright green, sometimes slightly yellow or cream, and occasionally have a scent that is a little like that of flowering currant (*Ribes sanguineum*). The plant grows wild in much of Greece, Macedonia and Serbia, Albania and southern Bulgaria. In gardens, it enjoys more sun than many species, but appreciates a rich, moisture-retentive soil. It is unusually susceptible to black spot and also to sudden spring frosts, damage from which can initiate black spot infection. Provide shelter from cold winds. The overwintering foliage of *Corydalis flexuosa*, early species crocuses, pushkinias, scillas and grape hyacinths (*Muscari*) are good garden companions. Propagate by division as hybridizing with other species is likely.

Height: 55cm (22in); Spread: 45cm (18in)
Planting distance: 38cm (15in)
Hardiness zones: 6–8, but this varies with origin of seed

With its richly coloured green flowers and tough, vigorous habit, Helleborus cyclophyllus *is one of the best of the wild species for garden planting.*

Helleborus dumetorum

This short and unprepossessing, but quietly attractive, demure hellebore is not for gardeners requiring sparkling colour. The deciduous foliage is divided into about nine narrow segments and arranged to produce a horseshoe shape at the base of the leaf. The green flowers are the smallest of all the hellebore

Small-flowered and rather dainty, Helleborus dumetorum *is slow growing and is at its best in a small intimate planting with neighbours that are not too aggressive.*

species, usually not more than 3cm (1¼in) in diameter, tending to face downwards and carried in heads of up to six flowers. It grows wild over a wide area of Slovenia into Hungary, Austria and Romania. In gardens, it is best in rich, leafy soil and enjoys more sun than most species but is also happy in shade. This is a slow-growing species that rarely makes extensive clumps. Beware of planting near overpowering neighbours; primroses and dwarf bulbs make good companions. Propagate by division as hybridizing with other species is likely.

Height: 30cm (12in); Spread: 23cm (9in)
Planting distance: 23cm (9in)
Hardiness zones: 6–8

Helleborus × ericsmithii

This variable but invaluable plant for both flowers and foliage has three broad divisions to each leaf. At their best, these are dark green with a spiny edge and pale veins; there may be pink tints in some plants. The flowers are up to 10cm (4in) across. They are usually pale pink or white inside, often with a central

green stripe in each petal, and darker and more often green- or pink-tinted on the reverse. It is another apparently unlikely hybrid, derived from *H. niger* and *H. × sternii*, and was formerly known as *H. × nigristern*. The qualities of its parents are combined in varying degrees, which leads to a range of features. At its best this is an excellent evergreen foliage plant, with long lasting flowers. *H. × ericsmithii* is an excellent garden plant for rich, well-drained soils, preferably with at least half a day's sunshine. It also makes a fine container plant, but it is also good in a low raised bed; remove much of the older foliage in autumn as a precaution against black spot. It looks good with a wide range of dwarf bulbs. Propagate by division, as the plants are sterile.

Height: 30–35cm (12–14in); Spread: 45cm (18in)
Planting distance: 38cm (15in)
Hardiness zones: 8–9

Helleborus foetidus

Commonly known as the stinking hellebore or bear's foot hellebore, this is a valuable and easy-to-grow British native, available in an increasing range of forms. It is a striking caulescent species, and each year an increasing number of stems develop from a slowly spreading rootstock. The stems carry bold, narrowly divided, slightly toothed, evergreen foliage, which is often rather leaden green and gives a slightly unpleasant odour when bruised. Each leaf is usually divided into about 12 leaflets. From midwinter to late spring, the stems are topped with up to about 40 tubular green flowers, 2cm (¾in) across, which flare with age. They are rimmed with reddish purple at the petal tips. The leafy bracts in the flowerheads are a notable feature in some cultivars, and the combination of upright stems, dark divided leaves and crowded heads of small pendulous flowers is instantly recognizable. The stinking hellebore grows naturally in Britain eastwards to Switzerland, and south to Portugal and the Balearic Islands. In Britain, it is usually found in woodland clearings and on the shady side of hedges; in southern Europe, short plants can often be found on sunny hillsides, which indicates its tolerance of a range of garden situations. It is, however, happiest in good soil

'Tros os Montes' is a tall and vigorous cultivar of Helleborus foetidus, *without the distinctive purple tip to the flowers seen in most forms.*

in partial shade, but will also produce creditable specimens in dry shade. The plant is relatively short-lived and support of lush specimens with slim bamboo canes may be necessary. In wet seasons and wet areas, precautions against black spot will be necessary. To maintain the display, snip off old leaves as they turn brown and cut out flowering stems at the base after flowering or seeding; this will also help to prevent black spot spread. This plant is impressive over a long period, first with its foliage, then with its late winter and spring flowers. It looks good backed by shrubs, as a specimen in an otherwise summer-flowering herbaceous border or with white daffodils (*Narcissus*), pulmonarias and a wide range of other shade lovers. Propagation is generally by seed only.

Height: 60–90cm (24–36in); Spread: 1–1.2m (3-4ft)

Planting distance: 60cm (24in)

Hardiness zones: 3–9

'Chedglow' is a slow-growing cultivar with golden yellow foliage. It is a shy seeder and susceptible to black spot, but dramatic in winter.

'Gold Bullion' is very similar to 'Chedglow', although possibly more vigorous and robust.

'Green Giant' is tall, up to 1.5m (5ft) tall, with pale, finely divided foliage and pale bracts.

from Italy is another tall form, 1.5m (5ft) tall, with more finely divided foliage and an unusually large number of flowers on each stem. It is very similar, if not identical, to Bowles' form.

'Marlene' is a North American cultivar with unusually finely cut foliage.

'Miss Jekyll' is one name for the *H. foetidus* form with scented flowers, which is sometimes listed. The leaflets are unusually narrow and the flowers sweetly scented, although not always consistently so. It is sometimes listed as 'Miss Jekyll's Scented Form' or simply scented form.

'Piccadilly' is a North American form with noticeably shiny, blackish green foliage and pale, whitish green flowers. There are reddish markings on the flower stems and leaf axils.

'Red Silver' is another North American cultivar, which combines rather silvery tints of 'Sopron' and the reddish tints of Wester Flisk Group.

'Sienna' has very dark, blackish green foliage. The flowerheads are large, bold and upright.

'Silvertooth' is a North American form with dramatic, unusually silvery foliage.

'Sopron' has dark metallic green foliage and unusually large, pale flowers without the reddish markings towards the petal tips.

'Tros os Montes' has large and dark, serrated leaves and pale flowers without the dark markings at the lip.

Wester Flisk Group is an impressive plant when at its best, with red-tinted main stems and leaf stems, with the staining continuing up into the flowerheads. It is variable, with uncoloured seedlings sometimes masquerading under this name. It is said to be even hardier than the normal species.

Helleborus hybridus

Commonly known as Lenten rose or Oriental hybrids, *H. hybridus* is the botanical name now favoured for all the popular, colourful hybrids involving *H. orientalis* and other species in its group (see 'Hellebore classification', p.14). It is a very large and diverse group of plants that shares the characteristics of bold, dark green evergreen foliage and upright flower stems carrying usually four or five flowers from 5–10cm (2–4in) across. The main species that have contributed to the development of this group include *H. orientalis*, *H. torquatus* and *H. odorus*.

Colours range from white through cream to primrose yellow, from blushed white through the full range of rose-pinks, peachy shades and various reds, and from misty mauves, deep plum purples, slate blues to almost black. Double-flowered forms of all these are becoming available as well as anemone-centred forms. All colours are also available with varying degrees of spotting on the insides of the petals.

Orientalis Hybrids are vigorous, tough and adaptable plants, which will grow in sun or shade. Their only demands are correspondingly more moisture in the soil to compensate for more exposure to sun. Forms available to gardeners fall into two groups; named clones propagated by division and named strains raised from seed. The former are relatively hard to find, owing to the slow rate of increase of individual plants; by the time sufficient stocks are available for nurseries to list them, they may have been overtaken in quality by seed-raised strains.

The large, smoky crimson flowers of Helleborus hybridus *'Garnet', raised by Helen Ballard, are the result of many years of careful breeding work.*

The latter are created by the controlled pollination, sometimes by hand, of carefully selected parent plants to achieve a desired result. Consistent seed-raised strains in particular colours are listed below, and these are the most dependable source of good garden hellebores. A number of specialists have their own strains, which are not listed individually. When choosing, look for balanced flowers with equal-sized, slightly overlapping petals that all share the same markings, if any; some are starry and some are evenly rounded, but unevenly patterned flowers are the least effective. Look for clear colours, since green tints can ruin good pure whites and clean pinks. The plants should also be prolific. Whether you like flowers that hang their heads or face outwards is a personal preference, and such characteristics are not always consistent from year to year. It pays to cut much of the foliage away in late autumn to help prevent black spot.

Picotees like this delightful form with its crimson nectaries are now becoming more widely available.

Height: 30–45cm (12–18in); Spread: 60cm (24in)
Planting distance: 45cm (18in)
Hardiness zones: 4–9

Named clones of *H. hybridus* propagated by division

'Apple Blossom' is a name used first by Margery Fish, then by Beth Chatto and more recently by others to describe forms with blush pink flowers which are sometimes spotted.

These hellebores are sometimes also seed-raised plants.

'**Cheerful**' has very impressive bright yellow, nicely rounded flowers.

'**Dusk**' has deep smoky purple flowers, slightly paler towards the edges.

'**Garnet**' has deep purple-red flowers, veined in black on the backs.

'**Günther Jürgl**' is a double form with green, pink-streaked backs to the petals, and the inner petals vary from green to pale pink with purple spots. The overall impression is of a pink-spotted double.

'**Little Black**' has evenly deep purple flowers, not more than 8cm (3in) across.

The spotted hellebores are universal favourites and this spotted pink form of Helleborus hybridus *has the added quality of even spotting across the petals.*

'**Philip Ballard**' has small, dark smoky blue flowers, slightly purplish on the insides.

'**Picotee**' is a name used for a variety of forms from a variety of sources, and is sometimes raised from seed. In common, they all have pale flowers with purple edging to the petals, and sometimes there are purple veins and purple nectaries.

'**Queen of the Night**' has deep purple flowers with purple-tipped, honey-green nectaries. Similar seed-raised plants are sometimes sold as Queen of the Night strain.

'**Snow Queen**' is vigorous with large, double white flowers. It is a parent of some of the large-flowered doubles now becoming available.

'**Sunny**' has pale cream flowers opening from yellow buds.

'**Ushba**' has pure white, rounded flowers with a very few small red spots.

Strains of *H. hybridus* raised from seed

A number of breeders and nurseries have developed their own seed strains in separate colours. These are in a constant state of development as improved plants are added to the parentage. Mostly, these are simply known by their colour, and plants that are listed as the same colour coming from different sources will probably be slightly different. Plants listed as the same colour from the same source may or may not vary according to the quality of the strain. Seed-raised plants can be unpredictable. Unless definite information on the precise colour of plants is available from the supplier, it pays to visit the nursery yourself and select these hellebores when they are in flower.

anemone-centred includes plants in which the nectaries have become enlarged and coloured to form a noticeable ruff around the centre of the flower. They are available in various colours and colour combinations.

Ballard's Group is a name used for any plants, in any colour, derived from cultivars or unnamed seedlings raised by Helen Ballard. Sometimes they are divisions of good-quality Ballard plants, and sometimes they are unpredictable, open-pollinated seedlings. They are understandably variable and unpredictable.

Anemone-centred forms of Helleborus hybridus, *in which the nectaries around the centre of the flower have become slightly enlarged and coloured, are becoming increasingly offered by nurseries.*

Heavily splashed yellow forms of Helleborus hybridus *are dramatic and colourful; the best forms have the spots equally distributed on each petal.*

DLC Hybrids include a wide-ranging blend of colours, from hand-pollinated parents.

double includes plants with double flowers with up to about 30 petals and usually no nectaries at all. They are increasingly available in a range of colours.

Elizabeth Town strain are lush, vigorous plants developed from Turkish seed. Their large flowers on stout stems range from purple-tinted pink to silver-pink with crimson speckling.

Kaye's garden hybrids is a name used to describe a range of colours raised by Reginald Kaye Ltd at Waithman Nursery.

Marion White Group includes very pretty, yellow-flowered doubles in the style of Party Dress Group, with red spotting on the insides of the petals.

'Moondust' has slightly starry white flowers, with an even red speckling and a clear white zone around the edges.

'Mrs Betty Ranicar' has blowsy, pure white, double flowers with a little green tinting at the base of the petals.

Party Dress Group are small, neat, pretty plants derived from double-flowered forms of *H. torquatus* and well-coloured forms of *H. hybridus*. They are sometimes slightly spidery in form, but become less so and more clearly coloured as the plants improve.

Royal Heritage Mixed has flowers 5cm (2in) across in a range of colours from white to maroon, with the emphasis on reddish shades.

Royal Heritage Slate/Smoky Purple has flowers ranging from dark slate blue to deep smoky purple.

Royal Heritage White has white flowers.

spotted includes plants with flowers spotted on the insides; the flower colour and degree of spotting varies.

'Stardust' has dark pink flowers with red spots, sometimes with green tints.

Winter Joy Applebud has light pink flowers.

Winter Joy Best Dark Form has flowers with deep red, purple and maroon tints.

Winter Joy Bouquet has flowers that range from creamy yellows to pale and strong pink to deep, very dark red on vigorous plants.

Winter Joy Creamy/White has white, cream or pale yellow flowers.

Plants in the Party Dress Group were the first double-flowered hellebores that were widely available; they come in a wide range of colours, this one is especially striking.

Winter Joy Pink/Dark Spots has pink flowers with dark spotting.

Winter Joy Spotted White has white flowers with red spotting.

Zodiac Group are pink-flowered plants with white margins around the edges of the petals, and an inner zone of bold reddish purple spots.

Helleborus lividus

This very attractive, short and neat species in the caulescent group is slightly frost tender. In habit, it is much like the more familiar *H. argutifolius*. The pink-tinted stems break from a very slowly spreading rootstock and carry neat, smooth-edged, bold leaves, which are divided into three leaflets. Each leaf is dark pewtery green with silver veins and pink undersides. The flowers are up to 3cm (1½in) across and appear from early winter to early spring. They are apple green or, in good forms, pink on the insides and pink or purplish pink on the outsides. The plant grows naturally only in Majorca where it has become very rare. In gardens, it hybridizes readily with *H. argutifolius* to create the variable *H. × sternii*. *H. lividus* grows best in gritty potting compost in a terracotta pot of 30–38cm (12–15in) in diameter or more for a mature plant. Mature specimens in pots make effective patio foliage plants during the summer months and can be brought into the protection of a cold greenhouse for flowering in winter. It can also be grown outside in a sheltered, sunny, well-drained raised bed in milder areas. It tends to be susceptible to black spot. This is naturally a relatively short-lived plant, so raise replacement seedlings after a few years.
Height and spread: 38cm (15in)
Planting distance: 30cm (12in)
Hardiness zones: 8–9

Helleborus multifidus

This group of four rather similar, green-flowered hellebore subspecies is generally more interesting than colourful. All are happy in dappled or partial shade in rich, but well-drained soil, and they appreciate protection from icy winds. They tend to

grow slowly. Propagate by division or seed, but guard against hybrids by planting away from other forms in this group.

Height: 25–30cm (10–12in); Spread: 30–38cm (12–15in)
Planting distance: 30cm (12in)
Hardiness zones: 6–8

H. multifidus subsp. *bocconei* has green, elderflower-scented flowers, which are pale to greenish white. These can be up to 7cm (2¾in) across, but usually less. The leaves are split into about 20 divisions, which may be elliptical or very slender, and are coarsely toothed. It is native to Italy.

H. multifidus subsp. *hercegovinus* is of most interest to gardeners, but is still rarely seen. The repeatedly dissected foliage can create over 100 divisions in a single leaf, which makes this an attractive foliage plant. It is also being used in breeding programmes to improve the foliage of *H. hybridus*. The pale green or slightly yellowish flowers are less impressive, usually less than 5cm (2in) across. It is native to Bosnia and Herzegovina. It may take some years for plants to develop impressive foliage.

H. multifidus subsp. *istriacus* has green flowers, up to 5cm (2in) across. They may sometimes be purple-tinted on the outsides. The foliage is the least divided of the four subspecies, with only about 12 broad leaflets, which have hairy undersides. It is native to an area on both sides of the Italy/Slovenia border.

H. multifidus subsp. *multifidus* has dark green flowers up to 3cm (1½in) across, and the leaves are each divided into 30–40 slender, toothed leaflets. It is found naturally in the coastal mountains of Slovenia and Croatia.

Helleborus niger

The Christmas rose is the most famous of the hellebores, with pure white flowers, but it is not the easiest to grow. It makes a short, evergreen plant with dark green, rather leathery foliage divided into seven to nine segments, which may be toothed towards the tips. The flat flowers can be up to 8cm (3in) across, more in some cultivars, and are held on stout stems between midwinter and early spring; usually white, they can also be tinted in various shades of pink. The foliage often overtops the flowers. The Christmas rose is found in the wild over

mountainous areas of Switzerland, southern Austria, Germany, Slovenia, Croatia and also northern Italy. It is one of the more difficult species to grow well, and prefers a partially shaded site on alkaline (limy) soil. In particular, it appreciates a deep, well-drained soil rich in organic matter, but with no shortage of moisture. Even so, it rarely seems to have the longevity of *H. hybridus*. It can be prone to black spot and is best treated as a specimen plant. Mulch well each autumn. Dwarf bulbs such as species crocuses, snowdrops (*Galanthus*), winter aconites (*Eranthis hyemalis*) and scillas make good garden companions.

Height: 30cm (12in); Spread: 45cm (18in)

Planting distance: 38cm (15in)

Hardiness zones: 3–8

Blackthorn Group are vigorous, seed-raised plants derived from 'Louis Cobbett' and 'White Magic'. The tall, reddish black stems carry pink buds that open to white flowers; they blush as they age.

Harvington hybrids have large white flowers, sometimes edged in pink, which stand up above the foliage. It is a seed-raised strain.

Plants of
Helleborus niger
Blackthorn Group
have crimson stems
and flowers that open
white with a slight
rose tint then fade to
dusky pink.

'**Louis Cobbett**' has very dark red stems with white flowers flushed pink on the backs.

H. niger subsp. *macranthus* has larger flowers compared with *H. niger* subsp. *niger*, and slightly blue-tinted foliage. It can be up to 45cm (18in) tall, occasionally more.

'**Potter's Wheel**' has pure white flowers 10–13cm (4–5in) across, with overlapping petals. It is a seed-raised strain with many impostors sharing the same name.

Sunrise Group has white or pale pink flowers, sometimes with creamy tints, and sometimes faintly striped.

Sunset Group has flowers that open white then change to deep pink as they age.

'**White Magic**' is a prolific seed-raised strain with unusually small foliage. It is one of the best garden forms of *H. niger*.

Helleborus x *nigercors*

This excellent and prolific, long-flowering hybrid combines features from both its parents (*H. niger* and *H. argutifolius*) to create one of the best garden hellebores. It quickly makes a broad clump with matt green foliage, each leaf split into three bold and broad, evenly toothed segments. The flowers appear from midwinter to mid-spring and are usually rather flat and

Combining the
qualities of the
Christmas rose,
Helleborus niger,
and the Corsican
hellebore,
H. argutifolius,
H. × nigercors *is a*
long flowering,
vigorous and easy
garden plant.

about 8–10cm (3–4in) across. They may be white, green-tinted or rather creamy, often with a green stripe down the centre of each petal, and they age to green and often develop pretty peachy tints in the process. Each flower maintains its appeal for an unusually long time. They appear singly or in twos, or in taller and more generous clusters. *H.* × *nigercors* is happy in a range of garden conditions from full sun to shade, and in most soils. Generous soil preparation ensures vigorous growth and a long and prolific season. It pays to cut much of the foliage away in late autumn, as with *H. hybridus,* to help prevent black spot and to ensure that the flowers are revealed. The flowers are unusual in lasting well when cut, even though the fat stems are rather short. Dwarf bulbs set around the original when it is planted will soon be absorbed into the clump as it spreads; they will then peep through among the hellebore flowers. Propagate by division in early autumn, although it pays to leave the plants to mature into a large clump. The plant is sterile, so there are no seeds.

Height: 38cm (15in); Spread: 60cm (24in)
Planting distance: 45cm (18in)
Hardiness zones: 7–9

Helleborus odorus

This easy and attractive hellebore is one of the more imposing species. The young foliage is covered with silvery, slightly coppery hairs. Each leaf expands into five main divisions; the outer divisions split again to give about 10 divisions in all. The foliage often overwinters, but may look tatty. The scented green flowers may be a bright pure green or more yellowish, and they can be as large as 6cm (2½in) across, opening from early winter until early spring. Their scent is variable, sometimes absent; sometimes it is said to be sweet or like elderflower, and other times it is less pleasant. *H. odorus* grows wild in Bulgaria, Romania and the more northern parts of former Yugoslavia. In gardens, it is generally easy to grow, doing well in full sun if the soil does not become too dry, but it also enjoys partial shade. It soon makes a big clump, flowering early and often setting a great deal of seed. The plant looks excellent with winter willows (*Salix*) and dogwoods (*Cornus*), and blue scillas or grape

Blood from the easy-to-grow Helleborus odorus, *a useful garden plant in its own right, has gone into developing the many superb yellow flowered forms of* H. hybridus *which are so admired today.*

hyacinths (*Muscari*) make ideal companions. Bronze-leaved forms of bugle (*Ajuga*) can be allowed to meander through the stems. It may cross with other species, so propagation by division is wise.

Height: 45–50cm (18–20in); Spread: 60cm (24in)
Planting distance: 45cm (18in)
Hardiness zones: 6–8

Helleborus orientalis

So many garden hellebores have been developed from this species, but it is not an especially valuable garden plant in itself. It is an evergreen perennial with large dark leaves split into seven to eleven roughly toothed divisions. The flowers appear from midwinter to early spring and are up to 8cm (3in) across, though generally less. The flowers of each subspecies are a different colour: greenish white, reddish white or white with spots. Usually, the markings are noticeably uneven across the petals. None of the three subspecies are especially effective as garden plants. All grow naturally in scrub, deciduous woods and by roadsides, usually in alkaline (limy) soils. In gardens, all three subspecies have proved to be tough, if unremarkable.

The one truly dependable Christmas flowering hellebore is this vigorous and resilient plant, Helleborus orientalis *subsp.* abchasicus Early Purple Group.

They thrive in shade, yet are happy in sun given sufficient moisture, and they are less fussy in alkaline soils. It pays to remove the leaves in the autumn as a precaution against black spot. Propagate by division as a guard against hybrids.

Height and spread: 45cm (18in)
Planting distance: 38cm (15in)
Hardiness zones: 4–9

H. orientalis **subsp.** *abchasicus* grows naturally in the Caucasus mountains. Its flowers are tinted red.

Abchasicus hybrids make rather short plants, about 30cm (12in) tall with dark pink to dark red flowers, often with an attractive grey-purple bloom on their backs.

Early Purple Group is a form of *H. orientalis* subsp. *abchasicus*, for many years known as *H. atrorubens*. These hellebores are dependably early flowering, almost always in early winter, and the flowers are more or less uniformly purple.

H. orientalis **subsp.** *guttatus* grows naturally in the Caucasus mountains. Its flowers are greenish white and very variably spotted in red or purple. Several good garden-worthy forms have recently been seen in the wild.

H. orientalis **subsp.** *orientalis* grows naturally along the Black Sea coast of Turkey. Its flowers are generally white with green tints.

Helleborus purpurascens

This relatively neglected hellebore makes a lovely early-flowering species when looking its best. It is one of the shorter species with deciduous foliage and flowers that may emerge in early winter. The leaves are hairy when young, developing a rounded outline. Their shape is unique among hellebores in that they are palmate (all the leaflets and divisions joined together at one point) rather than pedate (all divisions not joined together at the same point) like other species. The leaves of *H. purpurascens* are split into about 15 elliptical, toothed segments. The flowers reach up to 5–8cm (2–3in) across and start to open as soon as they peep through the soil. Their colour varies greatly. Some are soft purple outside and slightly paler inside, perhaps with a greyish tint, and some are misty purple outside and green within. Forms are also found in greyish blue,

At its best,
Helleborus
purpurascens *is not*
only a dependable,
if dwarf, garden
plant but also boasts
the most attractive
flower colours.

pinky purple or brownish shades. This hellebore grows wild over a large area of eastern Europe. In gardens, it enjoys good soil in full sun and also thrives in dappled shade. It is a great species for the front of a leafy border where the early flowers can be appreciated. Black spot may be a problem. Hepaticas, dwarf bulbs, *Lysimachia nummularia* 'Aurea' and bittercresses (*Cardamine*) make good garden companions. Propagate by division as a guard against hybrids.

Height: 30cm (12in); Spread: 38cm (15in)
Planting distance: 30cm (12in)
Hardiness zones: 7–8

Helleborus thibetanus

This very pretty but slow-growing, newly introduced hellebore from Sichuan province in China increases slowly. The leaves are split into seven toothed divisions and develop quickly in spring, but they tend to die down earlier than any other species. The unusually large-bracted flowers are bell-shaped at first, then flare open, up to 6cm (2½in) across, in late winter and early spring. They are white, or white with pink veins, usually fading

to pink, or pink darkening with age. This is a very pretty species for carefully cultivated woodland gardens in dappled shade with leafy soil. Dog's-tooth violets (*Erythronium*), choice trilliums, hacquetias and other special woodlanders make good garden companions. Many plants on sale in the West are collected indiscriminately from the wild, so check the source with suppliers and try to buy only nursery-raised plants. The seeds ripen earlier than most species, and on germination the seed leaves remain underground; development to a flowering-size plant is slower than many species. Early indications are that it will hybridize with a surprising range of other species. Propagate by division; raising plants from seed is very slow.

Height: 30–38cm (12–15in); Spread: 45cm (18in)

Planting distance: 38cm (15in)

Hardiness zones: 7–8

The most recent species to become available to gardeners is Helleborus thibetanus *with these elegant papery white flowers.*

Helleborus torquatus

This variable, but often very pretty species is the distant origin of many popular hybrids. It has deciduous, hairy foliage, which may be purple-tinted when young, maturing to a generally rounded overall outline. Each leaf may be split into as many as 80 divisions. The flowers are usually small, not usually more than

This form of Helleborus torquatus *brought the smoky colouring to some of the most appealing forms of* H. hybridus *and is a captivating garden plant in its own right.*

3cm (1½in) across, and there are several variations in colour: completely green, sometimes with pretty, dark veins on the insides; various shades of purple or brown on the outsides and green insides; and purple insides and outsides. The opportunities for confusion are obvious. It grows wild in much of former Yugoslavia. In gardens, this is generally a collectors' plant, as it is not sufficiently bright and colourful for less specialized growers. It grows slowly and is best grown in a leafy raised bed in partial shade, but it also grows in more sun in moisture-retentive soil. The plant is ideal with other choice woodlanders, such as wood anemones (*Anemone nemorosa*), snowdrops (*Galanthus*), primroses and trilliums. Propagate by division or by seed.

Height: 30–38cm (12–15in); Spread: 45cm (18in)

Planting distance: 38cm (15in)

Hardiness zones: 5–8

'Dido' is a double-flowered form found naturally in Montenegro with petals that have brown outsides and green insides. It is one of the parents of Party Dress Group.

double-flowered hybrids are descended from 'Dido' and another double form found in the wild called 'Aeneas'. The small, fully double flowers come in shades of green and brown. The name is sometimes used to describe

double-flowered hybrids with *H. hybridus* forms. See in flower before you buy to be sure of what you get.

Hybrids is a name usually used to describe seed-raised descendants of single-flowered forms collected from the wild. The flowers come in shades of green and brown, often with pretty internal veining.

semi-double is a name confusingly used to describe double-flowered hybrids with *H. hybridus*. See before you buy to be sure of what you get.

Wolverton hybrids are double-flowered forms also descended from 'Dido' and 'Aeneas'. The small, fully double flowers come in shades of green and brown.

Helleborus vesicarius

This unique and difficult, summer-dormant species has impressively inflated seed pods. It starts growing in late autumn and produces frost-tender, rather succulent stems. These carry bright green, juicy foliage rather like that of a buttercup or celery in shape. The leaves are also produced directly from the crown of the plant. In late winter, the neat, tubular green flowers open with a purple or brown band at the petal tips; they look very similar to those of *H. foetidus*. In early summer, the fruits mature and inflate to about 8cm (3in) in length. They are green at first then fade and dry before breaking off. *H. vesicarius* grows wild in northern Syria and southern Turkey, so it enjoys a Mediterranean-style life cycle. It appreciates moisture and protection from frosts while in growth, and a hot, dry spell in summer while it is dormant. The simplest way to achieve this is to grow it in a large terracotta container of well-drained potting compost. Keep the container in a frost-free greenhouse while the plant is growing and flowering, then move it outside for summer. Feed regularly while in growth; flowering may tail off on older plants, in which case they should be repotted using some fresh compost. The plant can also be grown in gritty soil in a glass-sided cold frame. Propagate by seed, which is a slow process.

Height and spread: 45cm (18in)
Planting distance: best planted individually in pots
Hardiness zones: 8–9

Helleborus viridis is a British native species which is more of a collectors' plant than an essential component of the winter and spring garden but is nevertheless a prolific species.

Helleborus viridis

The green hellebore is an interesting British native with a wide distribution across much of western Europe. It is a deciduous species, sometimes with purple-tinted young growth, and develops leaves that are split into five to seven main segments, and the outer segments further split to give around 20 in total. The dark green flowers are up to 5cm (2in) across. It is regarded as a collectors' plant because it is not particularly showy. It grows slowly and is best in light shade in alkaline (limy) leaf-rich soils; it also thrives in heavy clay. Propagate by division or seed, but guard against hybrids by planting away from other species.

Size: 38–45cm (15–18in); Spread 45cm (18in)

Planting distance: 38cm (15in)

Hardiness zones: 5–8

H. viridis **subsp.** *occidentalis* has hairless young foliage, and the mature leaves are coarsely toothed. In the wild, it has a more southern distribution.

H. viridis **subsp.** *viridis* has young foliage with slightly downy undersides, and the mature leaves are only finely toothed. In the wild, it has a more northern distribution.

FURTHER INFORMATION

All postal addresses and telephone numbers mentioned are correct at the time of going to press.

BOOKS

The Gardeners Guide to Growing Hellebores, Graham Rice and Elizabeth Strangman (David & Charles, UK, and Timber Press, USA, 1993)
Helen Ballard – The Hellebore Queen, Gisela Schmiemann and Josh Westrich (Eds) (Edition Art and Nature).
Hellebores, Brian Mathew (Alpine Garden Society,1989) Out of print
Hellebores by Marlene Ahlburg (Christopher Helm, 1993) Out of print

RHS AWARD OF GARDEN MERIT

The following hellebores have been awarded the RHS Award of Garden Merit:
Helleborus argutifolius
Helleborus foetidus
Helleborus niger
Helleborus × *nigercors*
Helleborus × *sternii* Blackthorn Group

For additions to the range of hellebores awarded the AGM go to the RHS website at **www.rhs.org.uk**.

The Orientalis Hybrids, Helleborus hybridus, *come in an increasingly wide range of colours – with and without spots.*

SOCIETIES

There is no hellebore society, but the British-based Hardy Plant Society caters generally for enthusiasts of perennials.

Hardy Plant Society, Little Orchard, Great Comberton, Pershore, Worcestershire, WR10 3DP. Tel: 01386 710317; Fax: 01386 710117; Email: admin@hardy-plant.org.uk; Website: www.hardy-plant.org.uk.

In the United States, The Hardy Plant Society, Mid Atlantic Group has a specialist group dedicated to hellebores and other shade lovers. **Hardy Plant Society,** MAG, 325 W. Ashbridge Street, West Chester, PA 19380. Tel: (610) 696 5503; Email: annhudnall@msn.com

PLACES TO VISIT IN THE UK

RHS Garden Hyde Hall, Rettendon, Chelmsford, Essex CM3 8ET; Tel: 01245 400256; Website: www.rhs.org.uk/gardens

RHS Garden Rosemoor, Great Torrington, North Devon EX38 8PH; Tel: 01805 624067; Website: www.rhs.org.uk/gardens

RHS Garden Wisley, Woking, Surrey GU23 6QB; Tel: 01483 224234; Fax: 01483 211750; Website: www.rhs.org.uk/gardens

Royal Botanic Gardens Kew, Richmond, Surrey TW9 3AB; Tel: 020 8332 5000; Fax: 020 8332 5197; Website: www.rbgkew.org.uk; Email: info@rbgkew.org.uk

Savill Garden, Crown Estate Office, The Great Park, Windsor, Surrey SL4 2HT; Tel: 01753 847518; Website: www.savillgarden.co.uk; Garden is at Wick Lane, Englefield Green, Surrey

East Lambrook Manor, East Lambrook, South Petherton, Somerset TA13 5HL; Tel: 01460 240328; Email: Elambrook@aol.com; Website: www.eastlambrook.com

Great Barfield, Bradenham, High Wycombe, Buckinghamshire HP14 4HP; Tel: 01494 563741

Old Rectory, Burghfield, Berkshire RG3 3TH; Tel: 0118 983 3200

Beth Chatto Gardens, Elmstead Market, Colchester, Essex CO7 7DB; Tel: 01206 822007

White Windows, Longparish, Andover, Hampshire SP11 6PB; Tel: 01264 720222

Gardens featuring hellebores which are open under the National Garden Scheme can be found by going to their website (**www.ngs.org.uk**) and searching for hellebores.

SUPPLIERS

In general, it is not possible for home gardeners to have hellebores sent from overseas although seed can usually be sent without problems.

United Kingdom

Jim and Jenny Archibald, 'Bryn Collen', Ffostrasol, Llandysyul, Dyfed SA44 5SB; Seed only

Ashwood Nurseries, Greensforge, Kingswinsford, West Midlands DY6 0AE; Tel, 01384 401996; Website: www. ashwood-nurseries.co.uk; Mail order for seeds only

Blackthorn Nursery, Kilmeston, Alresford, Hampshire SO24 0NL; Tel: 01962 771796; No mail order

Farmyard Nurseries, Llandysyul, Dyfed SA44 4RL; Tel: 01559 363389; Website: www.farmyardnurseries.co.uk

Fibrex Nurseries, Honeybourne Road, Pebworth, Stratford-on-Avon, Warwickshire CV37 9XP; Tel: 01789 720788; Email: sales@fibrex.co.uk; Website: www.fibrex.co.uk

Graham's Hellebores, Tel: 01594 860544; Website: www.hellebores.hort.net; No UK mail order; callers by appointment only

Harveys Garden Plants, Bradfield St George, Bury St Edmunds IP30 0AY; Tel 01284 386777; Website: www.harveys gardenplants.co.uk

North Green Seeds, 16 Wilton Lane, Little Plumstead, Norwich, Norfolk NR13 5DL

Paul Christian, Wrexham, North Wales LL13 9XR; Tel: 01822 855050; Website: www.rareplants.co.uk

Phedar Nursery, Bunkers Hill, Romiley, Stockport, Cheshire SK6 3DS; Tel: 0161 430 3772

Rarer Plants, Ashfield House, Austfield Lane, Monk Fryston, Leeds LS25 5EH; Tel: 01977 682263; No mail order

Europe

Gisela Schmiemann, Belvederestrasse 45a, D-90933 Koln-Mungersdorf, Germany; Seed only
Marlene Ahlberg, Hohes Feld 22, 38531 Rotgesbuttel, Germany; Seed only.

USA

For more detailed information on UK, US and other suppliers, please go to my website at: www.hellebore.com
Graham's Hellebores Website, www.hellebores.hort.net; US mail order from website only.
Heronswood Nursery, 7530 NE 288th Street, Kingston, WA 98346; Tel: (360) 297 4172; Website: www.heronswood.com
Pine Knot Farms, 681 Rockchurch Road, Clarksville, VA 23927; Tel: (804) 252-1990; Website: www.pineknotfarms.com
Plant Delights Nursery, 9241 Sauls Road, Raleigh, NC 27603; Tel: (919) 772 4794; Website: www.plantdelights.com
Russell Graham, 4030 Eagle Crest Road NW, Salem, OR 7304; Tel: (503) 362 1135
Windy Hill Plant Farm, 40413 John Mosby Highway, Aldie, VA 20105-2827; Tel: (703) 327 4211; Website: www.windyhill.net

ONLINE INFORMATION: WEBSITES AND MAILING LIST

In addition to the nursery websites (see above), there is also the following online information:

www.hellebore.com Detailed information and pictures from Graham Rice.

www.sunfarm.com Plenty of pictures from Barry Glick, an American breeder and wholesaler.

www.cube.icestorm.net/hellebores Dedicated to the appreciation of hellebores.

www.maigold.co.uk/helle.htm Hellebores from 'Graham Leatherbarrow's Paradise Garden'.

www.nurseriesonline.com.au/PAGES/Hellebores.html Directory of Australian hellebore nurseries.

Hellebore Mailing List: Exchange information with other hellebore enthusiasts. Register at: **groups.yahoo.com/group/hellebore**

INDEX

Acknowledgements

Illustrations: Patrick Mulrey
Copy-editor: Simon Maughan
RHS Editor: Barbara Haynes
Proofreader: Rae Spencer-Jones
Index: Dorothy Frame

The Publisher would like to thank the following people for their kind permission to reproduce their photographs:

Graham Rice/GardenPhotos.com except pages 14 and 52 (judywhite/GardenPhotos.com) and page 42 (Ed Sheppard).